Good Housekeeping

101 EASY RECIPES
LOW-GI

101 EASY RECIPES
LOW-GI

Lynda Brown

COLLINS & BROWN

First published in United Kingdom in 2006 by
Collins & Brown Limited
151 Freston Road
London W10 6TH

An imprint of Anova Books Company Ltd.

2 3 4 5 6 7 8 9

Project editors: Nicola Hodgson and Carly Madden
Design manager: Gemma Wilson
Production controller: Morna McPherson
Copy editor: Kathy Steer
Nutrtional analysis: Jenny McGlyne
Designer: Abby Franklin
Indexer: Michèle Clarke

ISBN 978-1-84340-354-8

A catalogue record for this book is available from the British Library.

Reproduction by Anorax
Printed and bound by Craft Print International Ltd, Singapore

This book can be ordered direct from the publisher. Contact the marketing department, but try your bookshop first.

www.anovabooks.com

All the ingredients used in this book are readily available. When buying them, choose local free range or organic when you can. Organic oats, milk carrots, potatoes and eggs, plus many other staples are available from all supermarkets. When using zest of oranges or lemons, it's a good idea to also use organic oranges and lemons.

Contents

Foreword

I first heard about the glycaemic index (GI) diet a couple of years ago when it hit the headlines as the latest weightloss craze. However, it isn't one of those eating regimes that's been in fashion then gone out again. It's been a quiet revolution from when it was first developed over 20 years ago to help diabetics maintain blood sugar levels. The GI approach is based around eating food that releases energy slowly, so it reduces hunger pangs and cravings for high-sugar food because you feel fuller and more satisfied. More importantly, eating these types of food can help to stabilise the body's production of insulin. This is essential to help the one in four adults in the UK who suffer from insulin resistance or Syndrome X, which can lead to heart attacks, strokes and Type 2 diabetes. Even if you don't have this condition, what is so great about the GI approach, is that its common-sense approach can be applied to everyone. We've gathered together 101 recipes, from energy-boosting breakfasts to quick lunchtime snacks and quick family suppers. There are also some great dinner-party recipes, plus some easy desserts, cakes and biscuits. All the recipes have been triple tested in the Good Housekeeping kitchens to make sure they work every time. Enjoy!

Emma Marsden
Cookery Editor
Good Housekeeping

Introduction

The low-GI eating revolution is the latest development in nutritional understanding of the role that carbohydrates (carbs) play in our diet, and is a way of eating that has many health advantages. This book has been written to help you master the low-GI way to diet and health for yourself and your family. It makes GI simple and easy, and shows you how you can change to low-GI eating naturally and effortlessly, so much so that your family probably won't even notice!

Carbohydrates are important energy and good mood foods, and are an essential part of any healthy eating plan. As this book demonstrates the trick is to eat 'smart' carbs – carbohydrates which give you maximum rewards both nutritionally and energy wise. This, in essence, is what low-GI eating is all about. 'Smart carbs' also have the added attraction that they can both help you to lose weight if you need to, and maintain your weight if you don't.

Another bonus is that low-GI eating really is effortless. You need no special ingredients or rigid eating pattern. The low-GI way to health is comfortingly familiar, and is perfect for modern tastes and lifestyles. Nor does it take any extra time. Just to make sure, our recipes have been specially selected to be easy to prepare and cook. We've also included the nutritional breakdown for every recipe, and made sure that none have too many calories, so all you need to do is cook, sit back and enjoy.

Finally, low-GI eating is a wonderful way to add variety, taste and interest to your diet, and can be a great opportunity to change your life for the better. This book is divided into six chapters designed to make it easy to find the right recipe at the right time of day – whether you're looking for a tasty brunch bite, food for friends or for a treat. We hope you will be inspired by our recipes, and have fun creating delicious low-GI meals for you and your family.

Happy low-GI eating!

Lynda Brown

Essential know-how

What is GI?

GI stands for Glycaemic Index, and is a measure of how slowly or quickly carbohydrates in the food you eat break down to glucose in your body. It is glucose – the simplest form of sugar – that your body and brain uses as fuel, both in every living process and to provide you with energy. Whether you have too much, too little or a steady flow of glucose in your bloodstream is fundamental to your overall health, and is the key to weight control, how you feel emotionally, and whether or not you feel energised.

What are GI foods?

GI foods are carbohydrate foods, and any food that contains carbohydrate, either in the form of starch, sugar or fibre will have a GI ranking. Pure glucose produces the greatest rise in blood sugar levels. Because of this it has been given a GI rating of 100 and is used as a standard by which other foods are ranked. All other foods are ranked from 0–100.

- ▸ **High GI: 70–100**
- ▸ **Medium GI: 55–70**
- ▸ **Low GI: 0–55**

Note: Although the rankings are useful, because different foods affect GI levels, it is the overall balance of the foods you eat in a day which counts, not just individual GI values.

What's the difference between high- and low-GI foods?

High-GI foods break down quickly in the body, causing a rapid release of glucose (blood sugar) into your bloodstream. Foods high in processed starch such as white bread, highly refined breakfast cereals and pastries are all high-GI foods. Low-GI foods, by contrast, such as pulses, wholegrain foods and most fruit and vegetables, break down slowly, causing a steady and sustained release of glucose into the bloodstream.

Why are high-GI foods bad for you?

Releasing high amounts of glucose into your bloodstream causes your body to go into red alert – too much is harmful, and to produce high levels of insulin (which regulates glucose and enables excess to be stored as fat). The net effect is the familiar yo-yo of 'sugar highs' followed by 'sugar lows' (energy dips), sugar cravings, mood swings and general fatigue. In time, insulin resistance, diabetes and other severe illnesses can develop. It's also thought that, for various reasons, high-GI foods are counterproductive and actually stimulate the appetite, rather than curb it, and are a significant factor in weight gain.

Why are low-GI foods good for you?

Low-GI foods avoid all the pitfalls of high-GI foods. In addition, because often they are more nutritious, they are good value foods. Choosing them is the easy way to ensure your diet is a healthy one. Research also suggests low-GI eating results in a higher level of good HDL cholesterol, which helps to protect against heart disease.

How do I know which foods are low-GI or high-GI?

GI values have been worked out for most foods containing carbohydrates, and you can buy books that contain only this information. Some manufactured foods in supermarkets also have GI values printed on their packaging. However, for practical purposes, all you need to know is which foods are high-GI foods and which are low. To make it simple, the chart on pages 12-13 lists green (low-GI foods), amber (medium-GI foods) and red (high-GI foods) to help you plan your dishes and menus.

What about proteins and fats?

Protein foods (meat, poultry, fish and eggs) and fats and oils do not contain carbohydrates, and therefore have no GI values. However, this does not mean that you can eat as much of them as you like. The usual healthy eating rules apply. Both, especially fats, are energy-dense foods, and should be eaten in moderation, while your intake of saturated and processed (hydrogenated) fats should be kept to a minimum.

▸ **Dairy products that have lactose (milk and yogurt and some cheeses) have low-GI ratings.**

▸ **Protein and fats slow down digestion of carbohydrates, and lower its GI. This is why, for example, although they are energy dense foods, nuts and seeds are low GI.**

What about fibre?

The presence of soluble fibre in food, for example, in oats and in fruits such as apples and pears, lowers GI. This is one of the reasons why dried beans and pulses are star low-GI foods.

What else affects GI?

GI is a measure of the rate at which carbohydrates are digested. The following factors affect this rate, and therefore the GI value of the food:

▸ **Cooking, mashing and processing**
▸ **Acidity**
▸ **The amount of protein and fat present**
▸ **The amount of carbohydrate and fibre present**

What about low-GI weight-reducing diets?

Low-GI reducing diets, combined with exercise, have been shown to be very effective, and are thought to be one of the best ways to maintain your weight safely. They usually also incorporate a low-fat regime.

Low-GI foods: 0–55 GI

All green vegetables, onions and leeks

All salad vegetables, and herbs

Sprouted seeds and bean shoots

Raw/cooked carrots, artichokes, celeriac

Avocado

Sweet potatoes, yams

Apples, blueberries, pears, plums, soft fruit, strawberries, stone fruits – nectarines, plums, gages, peaches and apricots

Citrus fruits

Fruit/vegetable juices.

Dried apples, pears, apricots, mango, prunes

Durum wheat pasta – all kinds

Egg pastas and noodles

Glass and cellophane noodles

Grain breads containing whole seeds and nuts; pumpernickel bread

Stoneground wholewheat and rye breads

Stoneground oats, rolled oats

Nuts and seeds

All dried beans and pulses

Canned beans; sugar-reduced baked beans

Brown, red and wild rice

Bulgur, buckwheat, quinoa, amaranth, pearl barley

Breakfast cereals and mueslis containing whole (not flaked) grains; sugar-free mueslis, All Bran

Meat, poultry, and fish

Dairy products

Fats and oils

Plain milk & plain dark chocolate

Medium-GI foods: 55–70 GI

Basmati rice

Couscous

Polenta

Rice noodles

Beetroot, swede, winter squashes (pumpkins)

Sweetcorn

Tropical fruits*: banana, kiwi fruit, mango, paw-paw, pineapple

Cherries, grapes

Fresh dates

Dried cranberries, figs, raisins, sultanas

Sugar

Honey

Maple syrup

Most jams and preserves

Most chocolates

* Amber fruits have GI values in the mid-to-high 50s. All are valuable sources of nutrients, so do not let their GI ranking deter you from eating them.

High-GI foods: 70–100 GI

Processed breakfast cereals such as cornflakes, Rice Crispies, puffed grain cereals crunchies, millet flakes, instant porridge oats; some mueslis

Savoury and sweet pastries

Most cakes and biscuits; croissants, crumpets

Processed savoury and sweet snacks

Processed white and brown breads, white flour

Crispbreads, crackers, rice cakes and popcorn

Canned soft and sports drinks

Risotto, pudding, sticky and quick-cook long-grain rice varieties

Gluten-free pastas and some noodles

Potatoes in all forms: e.g. mashed, roast

Broad beans

Cooked parsnips

Watermelon

Dried dates

Liquorice

Benefits of a low-GI Lifestyle

▸ Allows you to eat all foods.

▸ Ensures you eat plenty of fresh, wholesome, healthy unprocessed foods.

▸ Keeps you feeling satisfied for longer, so avoids hunger pangs.

▸ Controls appetite by ensuring stable reduced levels of blood sugar and insulin.

▸ Banishes energy dips and mood swings.

▸ Maximises burning of fat by reducing blood sugar levels.

▸ Helps protect against diabetes and heart disease.

▸ Ensures steady weight loss.

▸ Results in a slimmer, more energised, healthier, happier you.

In the kitchen

Switching to a low-GI lifestyle requires no radical changes to your diet or daily eating pattern – indeed that is part of its attraction. Nor does it mean only eating low-GI foods. It simply means altering the balance away from high-GI foods to low-GI foods, which take longer to digest and thus make you feel fuller for longer, and getting into the habit, whenever possible, of serving low-GI foods at every meal. The good news is, making some very simple changes can make a huge difference. For example, just eating one low-GI food at every meal will mean glucose and insulin levels stay lower all day.

Top tips
The golden rule is that the more starch has been processed or cooked, the higher its GI is likely to be.

▸ **Reduce highly processed foods, such as white bread products, breakfast cereals and pastries, sugary foods, confectionery, cakes, biscuits and canned soft and sports drinks as much as you can.**

▸ **Substitute lower-GI equivalents of basic high-GI staples – bread, breakfast cereals, rice and potatoes.**

▸ **When you eat high-GI foods, eat them in smaller portions.**

▸ **Remember to always cook pasta *al dente*; overcooking increases its GI value.**

▸ **Combine high-GI with low-GI foods to slow down the rate at which high-GI foods are broken down, diluting their effects. Thus, if you do eat a high-GI food or dish eat a low-GI food or dish to compensate.**

▸ **Include lean protein/fresh vegetables/fresh fruit/vegetables/salads/ pulses/nuts and seeds, whichever is appropriate when you eat, so that you will always be eating low-GI foods at every meal.**

▸ **Acidity lowers the rate of digestion of high-GI foods, for example, using lemon, lime juice or natural yogurt, eating half a grapefruit for breakfast, using a vinaigrette/balsamic dressing for salads.**

▸ **Choose fresh fruit or fruit canned in natural juice instead of sugar.**

Get smart: know your carbs

The secret to adapting to a low-GI eating plan is to substitute high-GI carbs for better low/medium-GI carbs, most of the time.

Bread

✗ White and brown processed breads in all forms have the highest GI ratings.

✓ Wholegrain, Granary, pumperknickel and seed breads, stoneground wholewheat and rye breads, sourdough breads.

Breakfast cereals

✗ Processed breakfast cereals such as Shredded Wheat, Rice Crispies, instant porridge oats, puffed cereals, cornflakes and those high in added sugar or honey such as crunchies and cereal bars.

✓ Porridge made with traditional rolled oats or stoneground oatmeal; sugar free/low-sugar mueslis, All Bran.

Pasta

✗ As long as you eat smaller than normal portions, pastas generally are OK GI carbs, and only gluten-free pastas, and wheat and rice noodles are high GI.

✓ All kinds of durum wheat pasta; fresh pasta made with eggs; cellophane and glass noodles (which are made from pea and bean flours).

Rice

✗ Most varieties of white long-grain rice, including processed American long-grain, jasmine rice, and all short round varieties such as pudding, risotto and sticky glutinous rice.

✓ White and brown basmati, brown, red and wild rice.

Potatoes

✗ All potatoes, boiled, mashed, fried, instant etc.

✓ Boiled new potatoes (these are still high-GI, but are significantly lower than maincrop potatoes). Sweet potatoes, sweet corn and yams.

Sugar

Though it's sensible to use as little sugar as possible, the only form of sugar that is high GI is glucose. Table sugar (sucrose) and honey is medium GI; the sugar found in fresh fruit (fructose) is low GI. You can now buy low-GI fruit sugar to replace table sugar in tea and coffee and in baking from supermarkets. This is expensive but you need one third less. When baking with fruit sugar, reduce the cooking temperature by 25°C.

▸ **Chocolate: Generally, chocolates and bars tend to have medium-GI values. Because of their added sugar and fat, however, they are still indulgence foods. Dark plain chocolate, with a minimum of 70% cocoa solids is low GI. Plain milk chocolate is also low GI.**
▸ **Dried fruits: These are low – medium GI. The one exception is dates which are extremely high GI and have a GI value of 100.**

Low-GI Snacks

Everyone needs to snack sometimes. Resist the temptation to reach for the biscuits or processed snacks, and tuck into these healthy low-GI snacks instead.

▸ **Fresh fruit, nuts and seeds are ideal low GI foods. Make sure you take some of each with you when ever you go out, or travel.**
▸ **Dried apricots and prunes are delicious nutrient packed low-GI snacks, and are the perfect handy snack instead of sweets.**
▸ **Keep a dip and crudités, or some squares of cold frittata, in the fridge for emergency snacking. Good dips are mashed avocado (guacamole) and hummus. Mayonnaise blended with a little mustard and natural yogurt is excellent also.**
▸ **An avocado is a light meal in itself, highly nutritious – a good source of EFAs (essential fatty acids) and vitamin E – and will keep hunger pangs at bay. Spoon a little extra virgin olive oil or your favourite health oil into the cavity and enjoy.**
▸ **A couple of squares of dark plain (70% cocoa solids) is a permissible treat, and better than a sugary snack.**

Healthy living

A low-GI diet ensures you eat plenty of unrefined, good carbohydrates, and will play a significant part in keeping you healthy and energised. Incorporating low GI eating into a new healthy lifestyle, by following the 10 simple steps to health, below, will literally set you up for life and ensure you achieve maximum health and vitality.

10 easy steps to health

1. Water
Water is the elixir of life, and is nature's prime detoxifier. Aim to drink at least 1 litre per day, preferably 1–2 litres ($1^3/_4$–$3^1/_2$).

▸ **Start the day with a glass of hot water and lemon.**
▸ **Have a small bottle or a large glass of water of mineral or filtered water, by your side always, and sip regularly.**
▸ **Water at room temperature is easier on the digestion than ice–cold water.**
▸ **Bored with plain water? Flavour your water with a slice of lemon, lime or some peeled and chopped fresh ginger.**

2. Superfoods
For tiptop nutrition and long-term health, incorporate these foods into your regular eating plan.

▸ **Avocado**
▸ **Broccoli**
▸ **Carrots**
▸ **Cabbage**
▸ **Garlic**
▸ **Ripe tomatoes**
▸ **Sprouted seeds, for example alfalfa**
▸ **Watercress**
▸ **Winter squash (dense orange flesh varieties)**
▸ **Apples**
▸ **Apricots**
▸ **Bananas**
▸ **Bilberries**

- Kiwi fruit
- Lemons
- Pineapple
- Live, natural yogurt
- Miso
- Oats
- Sea vegetables, for example nori strips

3. Superfood good fats and oils

Fats are essential to all life processes, including cholesterol, which is vital for nerve communication and an essential component of the brain, nerve fibres and sex hormones. For this reason, a low-fat diet is not a good idea for long-term health. The trick is to substitute bad (processed hydrogenated and highly saturated fats) for omega rich good fats and oils found in oily fish, nuts and seeds, and to eat small amounts of other natural fats such as butter.

- **Eat 1-2 tbsp extra virgin cold pressed oils every day. Olive oil, hemp, linseed and specially blends of omega oils are especially good. Do not heat. Use them to drizzle over salads, vegetables and fish, and in dips.**

4. Vegetables, salads and fruit

Vegetables, salads and fruit are star performers in all healthy eating plans, including low-GI ones. Not only do they contain a storehouse of vitamins and minerals, but they help to keep the body at its optimum pH, which is slightly alkaline.

5. Eat regularly

Skipping meals leads to energy dips, stresses your system and is a sure-fire way to put on weight. Eating regularly keeps your body's physical and mental energy levels steady, avoiding hunger pangs and the need to snack.

- **Never skip breakfast; it's the most important meal of the day to set you up and it also sustains your energy levels through until lunchtime.**
- **It takes 20 minutes for your body to register it is full and satiated, so eat slowly, and take your time.**

6. Variety

Enjoy as wide a variety of foods as possible. This way you will ensure your diet contains all the health giving micronutrients it needs for optimum health. It also helps to avoid developing food intolerances to particular foods.

7. Exercise

Regular exercise is vital, and is a crucial ingredient in all low-GI weight reducing diets. It energises you, raises your metabolic rate, helps to maintain your correct weight, is a de-stressor, releases feel good hormones and helps you sleep better.

8. Stress less

Stress is a major modern disease and comes in all shapes and sizes, be it pressure at work, noise and traffic, or the constant barrage of environmental and electronic pollution. The body reacts to stress by putting the body on to red alert and your immune system is compromised. Learning to deal with stress, and removing stress from your life wherever you can is essential for your health.

▸ **Build some form of relaxation into your daily life.**
▸ **Learn simple deep breathing techniques.**
▸ **Reduce the hours you watch TV or work/play on the computer. Listen to soothing music instead.**

9. Sleep

Sleep is Nature's happy pill, the ultimate physical and mental reviver, and the secret to staying young. Take care of your sleep and your body and your immune system will take care of you. Make getting enough sleep a top priority.

▸ **Make your bedroom a peaceful haven.**
▸ **Avoid drinking coffee or too much alcohol in the evening.**
▸ **Wind down before you go to bed.**

10. Positive outlook

How you feel has a critical impact on your health and overall wellbeing. Cultivate an optimistic outlook and do something that makes you happy every day. Laughter is great medicine, and is completely free.

Start the day

Starting the day with a good low-GI breakfast is one of the cornerstones of healthy eating. If you're in the habit of missing breakfast, now is the time to change. Research shows that it is the most important meal of the day. People who miss out breakfast suffer more energy dips and loss of concentration, and are more likely to have weight control problems. Turn the page and take your pick from instant nutrient-rich breakfasts to lazy brunches.

Apple and almond yogurt

Toasted organic oats with berries

Low-sugar blueberry jam

Granola

Muesli

Organic porridge with mixed dried fruit

Cranberry and mango smoothie

Summer berry smoothie

Mango and passionfruit smoothie

Mushroom soufflé omelette

Bacon and egg salad

Tuna melt

Lemon and blueberry pancakes

Low-GI beans on toast

Apricot and hazelnut bread

Apple and almond yogurt

Serves 4

Hands-on time: 5 minutes, plus chilling time

Cooking time: none

200 cals, 8g fat (of which 1g saturates), 24g carbohydrate per serving

500g natural yogurt

50g (2oz) each flaked almonds and sultanas

2 apples

1 Put the yogurt in a bowl and add the almonds and sultanas.

2 Grate the apples, add to the bowl and mix together. Chill in the fridge overnight. Use as a topping for cereal.

▼ **COOK'S TIP**

Put the apples, lemon, sugar and water into a microwave-safe bowl, cover loosely with clingfilm and cook on high in a 850W microwave for 5 minutes until the apple is just soft.

Toasted organic oats with berries

Serves 4

Hands-on time: 10 minutes

Cooking time: 5–10 minutes

260 cals, 8g fat (of which 1g saturates), 37g carbohydrate per serving

25g (1oz) hazelnuts

125g (4oz) organic oats

1 tbsp olive oil

125g (4oz) strawberries

250g (9oz) blueberries

200g (7oz) Greek-style yogurt

2 tbsp runny honey

1 Preheat the grill to medium. Roughly chop the hazelnuts and put in a bowl with the oats. Drizzle with the oil, mix well, then spread out on a baking sheet. Toast the oat mixture for 5–10 minutes until it starts to crisp up. Remove from the heat and set aside to cool.

2 Slice the strawberries and put in a large bowl with the blueberries and Greek yogurt. Stir in the oats and hazelnuts, drizzle over the honey and divide among four dishes. Serve immediately.

▼ **COOK'S TIP**

Oats are a great low-GI food, as they are highly nutritious and have many health benefits. Studies confirm that nothing beats oats for a healthy heart – their soluble fibre soaks up cholesterol like a sponge, lowering cholesterol levels and helping to keep your arteries clear. They are especially rich in B vitamins, calcium and silicon.

Low-sugar blueberry jam

Serves 6–8
Hands-on time: 5 minutes, plus cooling time
Cooking time: 8–10 minutes
60–40 cals, 0g fat, 15-11g carbohydrate per serving

125g (4oz) blueberries
75g (3oz) golden granulated sugar

1 In a large bowl, mix together the blueberries and sugar. Microwave on medium for 8–10 minutes, stirring twice.

2 Cool, cover and store in the fridge. It will keep for up to two weeks.

▼ **COOK'S TIP**

Blueberries are not only delicious but contain powerful antioxidants that are very beneficial to health. Studies show they may help protect against ageing diseases, reduce high cholesterol levels and keep the gut and urinary tract healthy.

Granola

Makes 15 servings

Hands-on time: 5 minutes

Cooking time: 1 hour 5 minutes

260 cals, 15g fat (of which 4g saturates), 27g carbohydrate per serving

300g (11oz) organic porridge oats

50g (2oz) each chopped Brazil nuts, flaked almonds,
   wheatgerm or rye flakes, and sunflower seeds

25g (1oz) sesame seeds

100ml (3½fl oz) sunflower oil

3 tbsp runny honey

100g (3½oz) each raisins and dried cranberries

1 Preheat the oven to 140°C (120°C fan oven) mark 1. Put the oats, nuts, wheatgerm or rye flakes, and all the seeds in a bowl. Gently heat the oil and honey in a pan. Pour it over the oats and stir to combine. Spread on a shallow baking tray and cook in the oven for 1 hour or until golden, stirring once. Cool briefly.

2 Transfer to a bowl and stir in the dried fruit. Store in an airtight container – the granola will keep for up to a week. Serve with milk or yogurt.

Muesli

Makes 15 servings
Hands-on time: 5 minutes
Cooking time: none
190 cals, 8g fat (of which 1g saturates), 26g carbohydrate per serving

350g (12oz) organic porridge oats

50g (2oz) each chopped hazelnuts, flaked almonds

   and sunflower seeds

50g (2oz) wheatgerm or rye flakes

25g (1oz) sesame seeds

100g (3^1/$_2$oz) each raisins and chopped

   ready-to-eat dried apricots

1 Put the oats in a bowl and add the hazelnuts, flaked almonds, sunflower seeds, wheatgerm or rye flakes and the sesame seeds. Stir in the raisins and chopped apricots.

2 Serve with milk or natural yogurt. Store in an airtight container.

▼ **COOK'S TIP**

For extra omega fats, add 25g (1oz) organic brown linseeds. Pumpkin seeds (rich in iron and B vitamins) make another low-GI healthy addition.

Organic porridge with mixed dried fruit

Serves 4

Hands-on time: 5 minutes

Cooking time: 5 minutes

290 cals, 6g fat (of which 2g saturates), 51g carbohydrate per serving

200g (7oz) organic oats

400ml (14fl oz) milk

75g (3oz) mixture of chopped dried figs,

   apricots and raisins

1 Put the oats into a large pan and add the milk and 400ml (14fl oz) water. Stir in the chopped dried figs, apricots and raisins and heat gently, stirring until the porridge thickens and the oats are cooked.

2 Divide among four bowls and serve with a splash of milk.

Cranberry and mango smoothie

Serves 2
Hands-on time: 5 minutes
Cooking time: none
140 cals, 1g fat (of which trace saturates), 3g carbohydrate per serving

1 ripe mango
250ml (8fl oz) cranberry juice
150g (5oz) natural yogurt

1 Peel and roughly chop the mango and put into a blender with the cranberry juice. Blend for 1 minute.

2 Add the yogurt and blend until smooth, then serve.

▼ COOK'S TIP

If you're on a dairy-free diet or are looking for an alternative to milk-based products, swap the yogurt for soya yogurt. Soya is a good source of essential omega-3 and omega-6 fatty acids, and can help to lower cholesterol.

Summer berry smoothie

Serves 6
Hands-on time: 10 minutes
Cooking time: none
70 cals, trace fat, 15g carbohydrate per serving

2 large, ripe bananas, about 450g (1lb),

   peeled and chopped

145ml (4$\frac{1}{2}$fl oz) natural yogurt

150ml ($\frac{1}{4}$ pint) spring water

500g (1lb 2oz) frozen summer fruits

1 Put the bananas, yogurt and spring water into a food processor or blender and whiz until smooth. Add the frozen berries and whiz to a purée.

2 Sieve the mixture, using the back of a ladle to press it through. Pour into glasses and serve.

Mango and passion fruit smoothie

Serves 6
Hands-on time: 10 minutes
Cooking time: none
100 cals, trace fat, 25g carbohydrate per serving

4 passion fruit, halved

2 ripe mangoes, roughly chopped

2 ripe bananas, chopped

600ml (1 pint) freshly squeezed
  orange juice

1 Push the passion fruit flesh through a sieve into a bowl to catch the juice. Discard the seeds and put the juice into a food processor or blender.

2 Add the mangoes, bananas and orange juice and whiz until smooth. Pour into glasses and serve.

▼ **COOK'S TIP**

An excellent start-the-day smoothie, especially rich in vitamin C and beta-carotene.

Mushroom soufflé omelette

Serves 1

Hands-on time: 5 minutes

Cooking time: 7 minutes

340 cals, 30g fat (of which 15g saturates), 2g carbohydrate per serving

50g (2oz) small chestnut mushrooms, sliced

2 tbsp low-fat crème fraîche

2 medium eggs, separated

15g (½oz) butter

5 chives, roughly chopped

1 Heat a small, non-stick frying pan for 30 seconds. Add the mushrooms and cook, stirring, for 3 minutes to brown slightly, then stir in the crème fraîche and turn off the heat.

2 Lightly beat the egg yolks in a bowl, add 2 tbsp cold water and season with salt and pepper.

3 In a separate bowl, whisk the egg whites until stiff but not dry. Fold, very gently into the egg yolks. Be careful not to over-mix.

4 Heat an 18cm (7in) non-stick frying pan and melt the butter. Add the egg mixture, tilting the pan in all directions so the base is covered. Cook over a medium heat for 3 minutes or until the underside is golden brown.

5 Preheat the grill to medium. Gently reheat the mushrooms and add the chives. Put the omelette under the grill for 1 minute or until the surface is just firm and puffy. Tip the mushroom mixture on top. Run a spatula around and underneath the omelette to loosen it, then carefully fold it and turn on to a plate.

Bacon and egg salad

Serves 4

Hands-on time: 10 minutes

Cooking time: about 10 minutes

360 cals, 23g fat (of which 7g saturates), 14g carbohydrate per serving

4 eggs

250g (9oz) rindless smoked bacon

150g (5oz) cherry tomatoes

2 slices thick-cut sourdough bread,

    with crusts removed

2 tbsp mayonnaise

Juice of $1/2$ lemon

25g (1oz) Parmesan cheese

2 little gem lettuces

1 Heat a pan of water until simmering, add the eggs and boil for 6 minutes. Cool completely under cold water, peel and set aside.

2 Meanwhile, heat a griddle pan, then fry the bacon for 5 minutes until crisp. Remove from the pan, chop into large pieces and leave to cool.

3 Add the tomatoes and bread to the pan and fry in the bacon juices for 2–3 minutes until the bread is crisp and the tomatoes are starting to char. Remove from the heat, chop the bread into bite-sized croutons and set aside.

4 To make the dressing, put the mayonnaise in a bowl and squeeze in the lemon juice. Grate the Parmesan and add to the bowl, then mix. Season with pepper.

5 Separate the lettuce leaves and put in a large serving bowl. Cut the eggs in half and add to the bowl with the bacon, tomatoes and croutons. Drizzle the dressing over it, toss lightly and serve.

Tuna melt

Serves 2
Hands-on time: 5 minutes
Cooking time: 5 minutes
390 cals, 22g fat (of which saturates 7g), 28g carbohydrate per serving

2 slices granary, sourdough or wholemeal bread

2 tomatoes, sliced

75g (3oz) canned tuna in brine

2 tbsp mayonnaise

Dash of Worcestershire sauce

50g (2oz) Cheddar or Red Leicester cheese, grated

1 Preheat the grill. Toast the bread on one side then turn it over.

2 Divide the sliced tomatoes between each piece of bread.

3 Drain the tuna and divide between the two slices of bread. Spread the mayonnaise over the tuna and cover with the grated cheese. Sprinkle a dash of Worcestershire sauce on each. Grill until the cheese is golden and bubbling.

Lemon and blueberry pancakes

Serves 4

Hands-on time: 15 minutes

Cooking time: 24–32 minutes

270 cals, 9g fat (of which 5g saturates), 41g carbohydrate per serving

125g (4oz) wholemeal plain flour

1 tsp baking powder

$1/4$ tsp bicarbonate of soda

2 tbsp golden caster sugar

Finely grated rind of 1 organic lemon

125ml (4fl oz) natural yogurt

2 tbsp milk

2 medium eggs

40g ($1^1/_2$oz) butter

100g ($3^1/_2$oz) blueberries

1 tsp sunflower oil

1 Sift the flour, baking powder and bicarbonate of soda into a bowl, tipping in the contents left in the sieve. Add the sugar and lemon rind. Pour in the yogurt and milk. Break the eggs into the mixture and whisk together.

2 Melt 25g (1oz) butter in a pan, add to the bowl with the blueberries, then carefully stir everything together.

3 Heat a dot of butter with the sunflower oil in a frying panover a medium heat until hot. Add 4 large spoonfuls (about a third) of the mixture to the pan. After about 2 minutes, flip over and cook for 1–2 minutes. Repeat with the remaining mixture, adding a dot more butter each time.

Low-GI beans on toast

Serves 4

Hands-on time: 5 minutes

Cooking time: about 10 minutes

330 cals, 9g fat (of which 2g saturates), 48g carbohydrate per serving

2 garlic cloves

1 tbsp olive oil

400g (14oz) canned borlotti or cannellini beans

400g (14oz) canned chickpeas

400g (14oz) canned chopped tomatoes

2 rosemary sprigs

4 thick slices granary bread

25g (1oz) Parmesan cheese

1 Finely slice the garlic. Heat the oil in a pan over a low heat, add the garlic and cook for 1 minute, stirring gently.

2 Drain and rinse the beans and chickpeas, add to the pan with the tomatoes, and bring to the boil. Strip the leaves from the rosemary, then chop finely and add to the pan. Reduce the heat and simmer for 8–10 minutes until thickened.

3 Meanwhile, toast the bread and put on to plates. Grate the Parmesan into the bean mixture, stir once, then spoon over the bread. Serve immediately.

Apricot and hazelnut bread

Makes 2 loaves: (12 slices each)

Hands-on time: 20 minutes, plus rising time

Cooking time: 30–35 minutes, plus cooling time

120 cals,; 2g fat (of which 1g saturates), 23g carbohydrate per serving

450g (1lb) strong granary bread flour

1 tsp salt

25g (1oz) butter, diced, plus extra to grease

75g (3oz) hazelnuts, toasted and chopped

75g (3oz) ready-to-eat dried apricots, chopped

2 tsp fast-action dried yeast

2 tbsp molasses

400ml (14fl oz) water

Milk, to glaze

1 Put the flour into a large bowl. Add the salt, then rub in the butter. Stir in the hazelnuts, dried apricots and dried yeast.

2 Make a well in the middle and gradually work in the molasses and 400ml (14fl oz) hand-hot water to form a soft dough, adding a little more if the dough feels dry.

3 Knead for 8–10 minutes until smooth, then transfer the dough to a greased bowl. Cover and leave to rise in a warm place for 1–1¹/₄ hours or until doubled in size.

4 Preheat a large baking sheet on the top shelf of the oven at 220°C (200°C fan oven) mark 7. Knock back the dough, then divide in half. Shape each portion into a small, flattish round and put on a well-floured baking sheet. Cover loosely and leave to rise for a further 30 minutes.

5 Using a sharp knife, cut several slashes on each round, brush with a little milk and transfer to the heated baking sheet. Bake for 15 minutes, then lower the oven temperature to 190°C (170°C fan oven) mark 5 and bake for a further 15–20 minutes or until the bread is risen and sounds hollow when tapped underneath. Cool on a wire rack.

Quick bites

It's equally important to eat well throughout the day. These recipes have been chosen as ideal snacks or no-fuss side dishes. When hunger strikes, pick up one of these easy, nutritious options.

Sun-dried tomato dip

Beef tomatoes with bulgur

Veggie pitta

Lemon hummus with black olives

Stir-fried veg with crispy crumbs

Chickpea and chilli stir-fry

Chickpeas with tomato and green beans

Sardines on toast

Braised garlic cabbage

Smoked mackerel citrus salad

Quick crab cakes

Pasta with broccoli and chilli crumbs

Chinese style fish

Turkey and broccoli stir-fry

Spiced tikka kebabs

Spanish omelette

Sun-dried tomato dip

Serves 4
Hands-on time: 5–8 minutes
Cooking time: none
150 cals, 13g fat (of which 2g saturates), 6g carbohydrate per serving

50g (2oz) sun-dried or sunblush tomatoes in oil

4 tbsp olive oil

Juice of $^1/_2$ lemon

150g (5oz) natural yogurt

1 Drain the tomatoes and put into a food processor with the olive oil. Add the lemon juice and yogurt and whiz to blend.

2 Serve in a bowl with sticks of raw vegetables such as carrots, celery, cucumber and cauliflower to dip, or spread on chunks of bread.

Beef tomatoes with bulgur

Serves 4
Hands-on time: 10 minutes
Cooking time: 20–25 minutes
280 cals, 14g fat (of which 4g saturates), 27g carbohydrate per serving

125g (4oz) bulgur

20g ($^3/_4$oz) flat-leaved parsley

75g (3oz) feta cheese

1 courgette

50g (2oz) toasted flaked almonds

4 large beef tomatoes

1 tbsp olive oil

1 Preheat the oven to 180°C (160°C fan oven) mark 4. Cook the bulgur according to the packet instructions. Chop the parsley, feta and courgette and stir into the bulgur with the almonds.

2 Chop the top off each tomato and scoop out the seeds. Put on to a baking sheet and spoon in the bulgur mixture. Drizzle with the oil and cook for 15–20 minutes until the cheese is starting to soften.

Veggie pitta

Serves 1
Hands-on time: 8 minutes
Cooking time: none
370 cals, 10g fat (of which trace saturates), 60g carbohydrate per serving

1 wholemeal pitta bread

1 tbsp hummus (see page 46)

15g ($^1/_2$ oz) unsalted cashew nuts

Handful of finely sliced mushrooms

$^1/_4$ cucumber, chopped

Fresh watercress or mixed salad leaves

1 Split the pitta bread and spread with the hummus.

2 Fill the pitta with the cashew nuts, mushrooms, chopped cucumber and a generous helping of fresh watercress or mixed salad leaves.

▼ **VARIATION**

Diced ripe avocado can be added. It is rich in omega fats and is good for your skin.

Lemon hummus with black olives

Serves 4
Hands-on time: 15 minutes
Cooking time: none
310 cals, 21g fat (of which 3g saturates), 21g carbohydrate per serving

2 x 400g (14oz) cans chickpeas

1 garlic clove, (use fresh garlic
   when possible, see page 94)

1 lemon

4 tbsp olive oil

1–2 tbsp of water(optional)

25g (1oz) pitted black olives

1 tsp paprika, plus a little extra

1 Drain and rinse the chickpeas. Crush the garlic and put into a food processor with the chickpeas. Zest and juice the lemon and add to the processor. Whiz to combine. With the motor running, drizzle in the oil to make a thick paste. If the hummus is too thick, add 1–2 tbsp cold water and whiz again.

2 Spoon into a bowl. Roughly chop the olives and stir into the mixture with the paprika. Serve with a sprinkling of extra paprika, if you like.

▼ **COOK'S TIP**

Hummus will keep for a couple of days in the refrigerator. It makes a perfect lunchbox food. Eat it on seeded breads, fingers of wholewheat pitta bread, or serve with crudités.

Stir-fried veg with crispy crumbs

Serves 4 (as a side dish)

Hands-on time: 10 minutes

Cooking time: 20 minutes

130 cals, 9g fat (of which 1g saturates), 9g carbohydrate per serving

1 thick slice wholemeal bread, crusts removed

2 tbsp olive oil

1 broccoli head

1 large carrot

1 red pepper

4 anchovy fillets

1 Whiz the bread in a food processor to make breadcrumbs. Heat 1 tbsp oil in a large, non-stick frying pan or wok. Add the breadcrumbs and stir-fry for 4–5 minutes until crispy. Remove from the pan and set aside on a piece of kitchen paper.

2 Cut the broccoli into small florets and chop up the stalk. Peel the carrot and cut into thin batons. Cut the red pepper into quarters, remove the stalk and seeds and cut the pepper into strips. Chop the anchovy fillets into small pieces.

3 Heat the remaining oil in the frying pan until hot. Add the broccoli, carrot and pepper and stir-fry over a high heat for 4–5 minutes until they're starting to soften. Add the anchovies and continue to cook for a further 5 minutes until slightly softened. Serve the vegetables immediately, scattered with the breadcrumbs.

Chickpea and chilli stir-fry

Serves 4
Hands-on time: 10 minutes
Cooking time: about 30 minutes
250 cals, 11g fat (of which 1g saturates), 28g carbohydrate per serving

2 tbsp olive oil

1 tsp ground cumin

1 red onion

2 garlic cloves

1 red chilli

2 x 400g (14oz) cans chickpeas

400g (14oz) can cherry tomatoes

125g (4oz) baby spinach leaves

1 Heat the oil in a wok. Add the ground cumin and fry for 1–2 minutes. Slice the onion and add to the wok. Stir-fry for 5–7 minutes.

2 Meanwhile, finely chop the garlic. Deseed and finely chop the chilli. Add to the wok and fry for 2 minutes. Wash your hands thoroughly after handling the chilli.

3 Drain and rinse the chickpeas and add to the wok with the tomatoes. Reduce the heat and simmer for 20 minutes. Add the spinach and stir to wilt. Serve with rice.

▼ **COOK'S TIP**

- Chillies vary enormously in strength, from quite mild to blisteringly hot, depending on the type of chilli and it's ripeness. Taste a small piece first to check it's not too hot for you.
- Be extremely careful when handling chillies not to touch or rub you eyes with your fingers, as they will sting. Wash knives immediately after handling chillies for the same reason. As a precaution, use rubber gloves when preparing them if you prefer.

Chickpeas with tomato and green beans

Serves 4

Hands-on time: 10 minutes

Cooking time: 15–20 minutes

300 cals, 14g fat (of which 2g saturates), 32g carbohydrate per serving

225g (8oz) green beans

2 medium onions

2 garlic cloves

3 tbsp olive oil

2 small green chillies (see page 49)

1 level tsp each ground turmeric,
   paprika and garam masala

1 level tbsp each ground cumin
   and ground coriander

4 tomatoes

2 level tbsp chopped coriander

1 level tbsp chopped mint

1 x 400g (14oz) can chickpeas

1 x 400g (14oz) can haricot beans

1 Cook the green beans in a pan of boiling water for 4–5 minutes until just tender. Drain well and set aside until needed. Finely chop the onions and garlic. Heat the oil in a pan with a heavy base, add the onions and garlic, and fry gently for 5 minutes. Halve, deseed and finely chop the chillies, then add to the pan with the spices. Cook, stirring, for a further 1–2 minutes.

2 Roughly chop the tomatoes and add to the pan with the chopped coriander and mint. Season with salt and pepper. Cook, stirring, for 5–10 minutes until the tomatoes are soft.

3 Drain and rinse the chickpeas and haricot beans. Add to the pan together with the reserved green beans. Simmer until the chickpeas are hot. Serve with roast chicken.

Sardines on toast

Serves 4

Hands-on time: 5 minutes

Cooking time: 8–10 minutes

220 cals, 8g fat (of which 1g saturates), 22g carbohydrate per serving

4 slices thick wholemeal bread

2 large tomatoes, sliced

2 x 120g sardines in olive oil

Juice of $\frac{1}{2}$ lemon

Small handful of parsley

1 Preheat the grill. Toast the slices of bread on both sides.

2 Meanwhile, slice the tomatoes and drain the sardines. Divide the tomato slices and the sardines among the toast slices, squeeze the lemon juice over them, then put back under the grill for 2–3 minutes to heat through. Snip the parsley over the toast and serve immediately.

Braised garlic cabbage

Serves 4 as a side dish

Hands-on time: 5 minutes

Cooking time: 6 minutes

110 cals, 7g fat (of which 1g saturates), 7g carbohydrate per serving

1 small Savoy cabbage, shredded

2 tbsp olive oil

2 crushed garlic cloves

Handful of chopped flat-leaved parsley

1 Heat the olive oil in a pan with a heavy base, add the garlic and cook for 30 seconds. Add the cabbage and cook, stirring, for 5 minutes. Season, stir in the parsley and serve.

Smoked mackerel citrus salad

Serves 4

Hands-on time: 10 minutes

Cooking time: 5 minutes

310 cals, 27g fat (of which 5g saturates), 4g carbohydrate per serving

200g (7oz) green beans

200g (7oz) smoked mackerel fillets

125g (4oz) mixed watercress, spinach and rocket

4 spring onions, sliced

1 ripe avocado, halved, stoned and sliced

1 tbsp olive oil

1 tbsp chopped coriander

Zest and juice of 1 organic orange

1 Preheat the grill to medium. Blanch the green beans in boiling water for 4–5 minutes until they are just tender, then drain well. Refresh under cold running water and tip into a bowl.

2 Grill the mackerel for 2 minutes until warmed through. Discard the skin and cut the flesh into bite-sized pieces. Add the fish to the bowl together with the salad leaves, spring onions and avocado.

3 In a separate bowl, mix the oil with the coriander, orange zest and juice. Pour it over the salad, toss together well and serve immediately.

Quick crab cakes

Serves 4

Hands-on time: 15 minutes

Cooking time: 6 minutes

130 cals, 6g fat (of which 1g saturates), 7g carbohydrate per serving

200g (7oz) fresh crabmeat

2 spring onions, finely chopped

2 red chillies, deseeded and finely chopped

  (see page 49)

Finely grated zest of 1 organic lime

4 tbsp chopped coriander

About 40g (1^1/$_2$oz) stoneground wholemeal

  breadcrumbs

1 tbsp groundnut oil

1 tbsp plain flour

1 lime, cut into wedges, to serve

1 Put the crabmeat in a bowl, then mix with the spring onions, chillies, lime zest and coriander. Add enough breadcrumbs to hold it together and form into four small patties.

2 Heat ^{1}/$_2$ tbsp oil in a pan. Dredge the patties with flour and fry on one side for 3 minutes. Add the rest of the oil, turn the patties over and fry for a further 2–3 minutes. Serve the crab cakes with lime wedges to squeeze over them.

Pasta with broccoli and chilli crumbs

Serves 4

Hands-on time: 10 minutes

Cooking time: 15–20 minutes

470 cals, 18g fat (of which 6g saturates), 64g carbohydrate per serving

2 slices wholemeal bread, crust removed

1 tsp chilli flakes

125g (4oz) smoked bacon

1 tbsp olive oil

300g (11oz) orecchiette pasta

1 large head broccoli

1 Put the bread into a food processor and whiz to make breadcrumbs. Stir in the chilli flakes.

2 Chop the bacon into small neat strips (lardons) and fry in a large frying pan for 5–6 minutes until golden. Set aside. Heat the oil for 1 minute and fry the breadcrumbs for 5–6 minutes until crisp.

3 Meanwhile, cook the pasta according to packet instructions; keep it *al dente*. Chop the broccoli into pieces, including the stalk. Add to the pasta 5 minutes before the end of cooking. When cooked, drain and return both to the pan.

4 Tip the bacon and breadcrumbs into the drained pasta, toss and serve immediately.

Chinese-style fish

Serves 4

Hands-on time: 10 minutes

Cooking time: 10 minutes

150 cals, 3g fat (of which 1g saturates), 12g carbohydrate per serving

2 tsp sunflower oil

1 small onion, finely chopped

1 green chilli, deseeded and finely chopped

2 courgettes, thinly sliced

125g (4oz) frozen peas (defrosted)

350g (12oz) skinless haddock fillet,

   cut into bite-sized pieces

2 tsp lemon juice

4 tbsp hoisin sauce

1 Heat the oil in a large, non-stick frying pan. Add the onion, chilli, courgettes and peas. Stir over a high heat for 5 minutes until the vegetables begin to soften.

2 Add the fish to the pan with the lemon juice, hoisin sauce and 150ml (¼ pint) water. Bring to the boil, then simmer, uncovered, for 2–3 minutes or until the fish is cooked through.

Turkey and broccoli stir-fry

Serves 4

Hands-on time: 15 minutes

Cooking time: 7–11 minutes

240 cals, 9g fat (of which 1g saturates), 5g carbohydrate per serving

2 tbsp vegetable or sunflower oil

500g (1lb 2oz) turkey fillet, cut into strips

2 garlic cloves, crushed

2.5cm (1in) piece fresh root ginger, grated

1 broccoli head, chopped into florets

8 spring onions, finely chopped

125g (4oz) button mushrooms, halved

100g (3½oz) beansprouts

3 tbsp oyster sauce

1 tbsp light soy sauce

125ml (4fl oz) hot chicken stock

Juice of ½ organic lemon

1 Heat 1 tbsp oil in a large, non-stick frying pan or wok, add the turkey strips and stir-fry for 4–5 minutes until golden and cooked through. Remove from the pan and set aside.

2 Heat the remaining oil in the same pan over a medium heat, add the garlic and ginger and cook for 30 seconds, stirring all the time so they don't burn. Add the broccoli, onions and mushrooms, turn up the heat and cook for 2–3 minutes until the vegetables start to brown but are still crisp.

3 Return the turkey to the pan and add the beansprouts, sauces, stock and lemon juice. Cook for 1–2 minutes, tossing well to heat everything through, then serve.

Spiced tikka kebabs

Serves 4

Hands-on time: 10 minutes

Cooking time: 8–10 minutes

40 cals, 2g fat (of which trace saturates), 2g carbohydrate per serving

2 tbsp tikka paste

150g (5oz) natural yogurt

Juice of $\frac{1}{2}$ lime

4 spring onions, chopped

350g (12oz) skinless chicken, cut into

   bite-sized pieces

Lime wedges, to serve

1 Preheat the grill. Put the tikka paste, yogurt, lime juice and chopped spring onions into a large bowl. Add the chicken and toss well. Thread the chicken on to skewers.

2 Grill for 8–10 minutes on each side or until cooked through, turning and basting with the paste. Serve with lime wedges to squeeze over them.

▼ **SERVE WITH**

Rocket salad: put 75g (3oz) rocket in a large bowl. Add $\frac{1}{4}$ chopped avocado, a handful of chopped cherry tomatoes, $\frac{1}{2}$ chopped cucumber and the juice of 1 lime. Season with salt and pepper and mix together. Serves 4 as a side dish.

Spanish omelette

Serves 4

Hands-on time: 5 minutes

Cooking time: 15 minutes

490 cals, 39g fat (of which 14g saturates), 8g carbohydrate per serving

225g (8oz) piece good-quality salami, chorizo

   or garlic sausage, roughly chopped

50g (2oz) stale sourdough bread (crusts removed)

roughly chopped

8 large eggs

2 spring onions, finely chopped

1 small bunch chives, or any other fresh herbs

   you fancy, finely chopped

1 Heat a large, 28cm (11in), frying pan with a heavy base, add the salami or chorizo pieces and fry over a low heat until the fat begins to run. Increase the heat and cook the meat until golden and crisp. Remove from the pan (leaving the fat in the pan) and set aside. Add the bread to the pan and fry until it's also golden and crisp. Remove the pan from the heat, mix the croutons with the cooked salami and keep warm until needed.

2 In a bowl, beat together the eggs, spring onions and chives, then season with pepper. Heat the fat in the pan used for the salami and bread. When very hot, add the egg mixture, allowing the liquid to spread across the base of the pan. Cook for 2 minutes, then, using a spatula, draw the cooked edges into the centre, tilting the pan so the mixture runs into the gaps.

3 When the omelette is almost set, reduce the heat and spoon the salami and crouton mixture evenly over the top. Cook for a further 30 seconds, then cut the omelette into four wedges. Sprinkle with the herbs and serve with a green salad.

Soups and salads

Soups and salads add variety to your diet, and are great when you don't want to cook a full meal but need something light, simple and healthy. These dishes are perfect at lunchtime or in the evening; all are made using only fresh, natural ingredients and are low-GI.

Celery soup

Serves 4–6

Hands-on time: 10 minutes

Cooking time: 30–40 minutes

120–80 cals, 10–7g fat (of which 5–3g saturates), 5–3g carbohydrate per serving

25g (1oz) butter

1 tbsp olive oil

1 medium leek, sliced

6 celery sticks, finely sliced

1 tbsp finely chopped sage

600ml (1 pint) hot chicken stock

300ml ($^{1}/_{2}$ pint) milk

1 Melt the butter in a pan and add the oil. Add the leek and fry for 10–15 minutes until soft. Add the celery and sage and cook for 5 minutes to soften.

2 Add the hot chicken stock and milk to the pan, then season with salt and pepper, cover and bring to the boil. Reduce the heat and simmer for 10–15 minutes or until the celery is tender.

3 Leave to cool a little, then whiz in a food processor. Return the soup to the pan, reheat gently and season to taste with salt and pepper.

Fast fish soup

Serves 4

Hands-on time: 5 minutes

Cooking time: about 15 minutes

250 cals, 12g fat (of which 2g saturates), 3g carbohydrate per serving

1 leek, finely chopped

4 fat garlic cloves, crushed

3 celery sticks, finely chopped

1 small fennel bulb, finely chopped

1 red chilli, deseeded and finely chopped

  (see page 49)

3 tbsp olive oil

50ml (2fl oz) white wine

About 750g (1½lb) mixed fish and shellfish,

  such as haddock, monkfish, raw shelled

  prawns, salmon and cleaned mussels

4 medium tomatoes, chopped

20g pack fresh thyme, finely chopped

1 Put the leek in a large pan and add the garlic, celery, fennel, chilli and olive oil. Cook over a medium heat for 5 minutes or until vegetables are soft and beginning to colour.

2 Stir in 1.1 litres (2 pints) boiling water and the wine. Bring to the boil then simmer the soup, covered, for 5 minutes.

3 Cut the fish into large chunks. Add to the soup with the tomatoes and thyme. Continue simmering gently until the fish has just turned opaque. Add the prawns, simmer for 1 minute then add mussels – if you're using them. As soon as all the mussels have opened, season and ladle into bowls. Serve with granary or wholewheat bread.

Mixed beans and tomato soup

Serves 4

Hands-on time: 15 minutes

Cooking time: around 30 minutes

170 cals, 6g fat (of which 1g saturates), 23g carbohydrate per serving

1 large onion

2 garlic cloves

1 red pepper

3 celery sticks

1 tbsp olive oil

1 level tbsp sun-dried tomato paste

2 x 400g (14oz) cans chopped tomatoes

300ml (½ pint) hot chicken or vegetable stock

400g (14oz) can of mixed beans

1 Chop the onion and garlic. Thinly slice the pepper and celery. Heat the oil in a large pan, add the onion and garlic and cook over a low heat for 5–7 minutes or until the onion is beginning to soften.

2 Add the pepper and celery to the pan and continue cooking for a futher 5 minutes.

3 Stir in the tomato paste, tomatoes and stock. Cook over a low heat for 5 minutes.

4 Drain and rinse the beans and add to the pan. Simmer for 5 minutes and serve.

Carrot and sweet potato soup

Makes 2.4 litres (4 pints) to serve 8

Hands-on time: 15 minutes

Cooking time: 45 minutes

130 cals, 5g fat (of which 1g saturates), 22g carbohydrate per serving

1 tbsp olive oil

1 large onion, chopped

1 level tbsp coriander seeds

900g (2lb) carrots, roughly chopped

2 medium sweet potatoes, mashed

2 litres (3½ pints) hot vegetable stock or chicken stock

2 tbsp white wine vinegar

2 tbsp chopped coriander, plus extra sprigs to garnish

4 tbsp half-fat crème fraîche

1 Heat the oil in a large pan, add the onion and coriander seeds and cook over a medium heat for 5 minutes. Add the carrots and sweet potatoes, and cook for a further 5 minutes.

2 Add the stock and bring the soup to the boil. Reduce the heat and leave to simmer for 25 minutes. Cool slightly, then put in a liquidiser and whiz until slightly chunky. Add the vinegar and season with salt and pepper.

3 Cool half the quantity of soup, then freeze it. Pour the remainder into a clean pan, stir in the chopped coriander and reheat gently.

4 Divide the soup among four warmed bowls, then garnish each with 1 tbsp crème fraîche and a coriander sprig to serve.

Summer vegetable soup

Serves 4–6

Hands-on time: 45 minutes

Cooking time: 1 hour

250–160 cals, 12–8g fat (of which 2–1g saturates) 28–19g carbohydrate
per serving

3 tbsp sunflower oil

1 medium onion, finely chopped

225g (8oz) new potatoes, finely diced

175g (6oz) carrots, finely diced

1 medium turnip, finely diced

4 bay leaves

6 large sage leaves

2 courgettes, about 375g (13oz), finely diced

175g (6oz) French beans, trimmed and halved

125g (4oz) shelled peas

225g (8oz) tomatoes, deseeded and finely diced

1 small head broccoli, broken into florets

Ready-made pesto, to serve

1 Heat the oil in a large pan, add the onion, potatoes, carrots and turnip and fry over a low heat for 10 minutes. Add 1.7 litres (3 pints) cold water, bring to the boil and add the bay and sage leaves. Reduce the heat and simmer for 25 minutes.

2 Add the courgettes, French beans, peas and tomatoes to the pan. Return to the boil, then simmer for 10–15 minutes. Add the broccoli 5 minutes before the end of the cooking time.

3 Remove the bay and sage leaves and adjust the seasoning if necessary. Pour the soup into bowls. Remove 12 French beans, add a spoonful of pesto and garnish with the reserved french beans.

Hot and sour turkey soup

Serves 4

Hands-on time: 25 minutes

Cooking time: 40 minutes

210 cals, 6g fat (of which 1g saturates), 18g carbohydrate per serving

1 tbsp vegetable oil

300g (11oz) turkey breasts, cut into strips

5cm (2in) piece fresh root ginger, grated

4 spring onions, finely sliced

1–2 tbsp Thai red curry paste

75g (3oz) basmati rice

1.1 litre (2 pints) weak hot chicken or vegetable
   stock, or boiling water

200g (7oz) mangetout, sliced

Juice of 1 lime

1 Heat the oil in a deep pan. Add the turkey and cook over a medium heat for 5 minutes until browned.

2 Add the ginger and spring onions. Cook for a further 2–3 minutes. Stir in the Thai curry paste and cook for 1–2 minutes to warm the spices.

3 Add the rice and stir to coat in the curry paste. Pour the hot stock into the pan. Stir once and bring to the boil. Turn the heat down and leave to simmer, covered, for 20 minutes.

▼ **COOK'S TIP**

Red Thai curry paste is a hot chilli paste, if you prefer a milder version use Green Thai curry paste.

Tomato, pepper and orange soup

Serves 4

Hands-on time: 15 minutes

Cooking time: 12 minutes

120 cals, 1g fat (of which trace saturates), 28g carbohydrate per serving

3 fresh rosemary sprigs

400g (14oz) jar roasted red peppers, drained

2 tsp golden caster sugar

1 litre (1$^3/_4$ pints) tomato juice

4 very ripe plum tomatoes

300ml ($^1/_2$ pint) hot chicken stock

450ml ($^3/_4$ pint) freshly squeezed orange juice

1 Pull the leaves from the rosemary sprigs and discard the twiggy stalks. Put the leaves into a food processor, add the peppers, sugar, half the tomato juice and the plum tomatoes and whiz together until slightly chunky.

2 Sieve the mixture into a pan and stir in the stock, orange juice and the remaining tomato juice. Bring to the boil and simmer gently for about 10 minutes. Season with plenty of pepper to serve.

Winter leaf salad

Serves 10

Hands-on time: 20 minutes

Cooking time: none

110 cals, 11g fat (of which 2g saturates), 1g carbohydrate per serving

100g (3^{1}/$_{2}$oz) lamb's lettuce

1 heads radicchio

2 heads red chicory

125g (4oz) walnuts, toasted and roughly chopped

for the dressing

2 tbsp white wine vinegar

2 tbsp walnut oil

4 tbsp olive oil

1 Put the dressing ingredients in a jam jar. Season with salt and pepper and shake well to mix.

2 Tear all the salad leaves into bite-sized pieces and put into a large bowl. Add the walnuts and toss to mix.

3 To serve, shake the dressing again, then pour it over the salad and toss well. Divide between two large bowls.

Tomato and olive salad

Serves 4

Hands-on time: 15 minutes

Cooking time: none

230 cals, 22g fat (of which 3g saturates), 7g carbohydrate per serving

700g (1$\frac{1}{2}$lb) ripe tomatoes

75g (3oz) pitted black olives

Small handful flat-leaved parsley

1 shallot or small onion

6 tbsp olive oil

2 tbsp white wine vinegar

2 level tsp Dijon mustard

1 Slice the tomatoes, roughly chop the olives and parsley, and finely slice the shallot.

2 Put the olive oil in a bowl. Add the white wine vinegar, mustard, shallot, parsley and a little salt. Whisk everything together.

3 Toss the tomatoes and olives with the dressing, season well and serve immediately.

Summer vegetable salad

Serves 10
Hands-on time: 10 minutes
Cooking time: about 10 minutes
70 cals, 4g fat (of which 1g saturates), 5g carbohydrate per serving

900g (2lb) mixed green vegetables, such as

  French beans, peas, sugar snap peas, trimmed

  asparagus, broad beans, broccoli

$1/_4$ cucumber, halved, deseeded and sliced

1 tbsp chopped flat-leaved parsley

for the dressing

1 tbsp white wine vinegar or sherry vinegar

1 tsp English mustard powder

3 tbsp extra-virgin olive oil

1 Cook the beans in a large pan of salted boiling water for 5 minutes, then add all the other vegetables. Return the water to the boil and cook for a further 3–4 minutes. Drain well and put immediately into a bowl of ice-cold water.

2 Whisk all the dressing ingredients together.

3 To serve, drain the vegetables and then toss in the dressing with the cucumber and parsley.

Chickpea and beetroot salad with mint yogurt dressing

Serves 4

Hands-on time: 15 minutes

Cooking time: none

240 cals, 9g fat (of which 1g saturates), 30g carbohydrate per serving

250g (9oz) cooked beetroot (without vinegar)

400g (14oz) canned chickpeas

50g (2oz) sultanas

20g ($^3/_4$oz) basil

1 medium carrot

$^1/_2$ small white cabbage

1 lemon

150g (5oz) Greek-style yogurt

20g pack mint

2 tbsp extra-virgin olive oil

1 Roughly chop the beetroot, drain and rinse the chickpeas and put both in a large bowl. Add the sultanas, tear the basil and add, then grate in the carrot. Finely shred the cabbage and add to the bowl. Halve the lemon and squeeze the juice into the bowl.

2 Put the yogurt in a separate bowl. Chop the mint and add to the yogurt with the oil. Season with salt and pepper. Spoon on to the salad and mix everything together. Serve immediately.

Smoked mackerel with potato and horseradish salad

Serves 4

Hands-on time: 15 minutes

Cooking time: 20 minutes

400 cals, 30g fat (of which 6g saturates), 22g carbohydrate per serving

350g (12oz) new potatoes, scrubbed

2 tbsp horseradish sauce

2 tbsp crème fraîche

1 tbsp lemon juice

4 tbsp olive oil

2 crisp apples

2 smoked mackerel fillets

100g (3$^{1}/_{2}$oz) watercress

1 Cook the potatoes in a pan of salted boiling water for 15–20 minutes or until tender. Drain and set aside.

2 In a bowl, mix together the horseradish sauce, crème fraîche, lemon juice and oil, then season with pepper. Roughly chop the apples and the warm potatoes, put in a large bowl and toss in the dressing. Skin and flake the mackerel and add to the bowl with the watercress. Toss together and serve.

Warm pepper and tomato salad

Serves 4

Hands-on time: 15 minutes

Cooking time: 45–50 minutes

210 cals, 17g fat (of which 2g saturates), 13g carbohydrate per serving

4 red peppers

3 tbsp olive oil, plus extra for greasing

400g (14oz) cherry tomatoes

2 tbsp chilli oil

1 scant tbsp soft brown sugar

2 tbsp balsamic vinegar

1 Preheat the oven to 180°C (160° fan oven) mark 4. Cut the peppers in half lengthways. Remove the seeds but leave the stalks intact. Put on a lightly oiled baking tray and fill each half with tomatoes. Drizzle with chilli oil and season. Cook in the oven for 45–50 minutes.

2 Meanwhile, put the sugar in a bowl and add the vinegar. Whisk until the sugar has dissolved. Gradually whisk in the olive oil and season to taste. Serve the peppers drizzled with the balsamic vinegar.

Bacon, avocado and pine nut salad

Serves 4

Hands-on time: 5 minutes

Cooking time: 7 minutes

430 cals, 42g fat (of which 8g saturates), 3g carbohydrate per serving

125g (4oz) streaky bacon rashers, de-rinded
   and cut into small, neat piece (lardons)

1 shallot, finely chopped

120g bag mixed baby salad leaves

1 ripe medium avocado

50g (2oz) pine nuts

4 tbsp olive oil

4 tbsp red wine vinegar

1 Put the bacon lardons into a frying pan over a medium heat for 1–2 minutes until the fat starts to run. Add the chopped shallot and fry gently for about 5 minutes until golden.

2 Meanwhile, divide the salad leaves among four serving plates. Halve and stone the avocado, then peel and slice the flesh. Arrange on the salad leaves.

3 Add the pine nuts, oil and wine vinegar to the frying pan and let bubble for 1 minute. Season with salt and pepper.

4 Tip the bacon, pine nuts and dressing over the salad and serve at once, while still warm, as a starter.

▼ **VARIATION**

Replace the pine nuts with walnuts.

Pasta and avocado salad

Serves 4
Hands-on time: 5 minutes
Cooking time: none
300 cals, 25g fat (of which 3g saturates), 14g carbohydrate per serving

2 tbsp mayonnaise

2 level tbsp pesto

2 ripe avocados, cut into cubes

225g (8oz) cooked pasta, cooled

A few basil leaves

1 Mix together the mayonnaise, pesto and avocados, then mix with the pasta. If the dressing is too thick, dilute with a little of the pasta water.

2 Decorate with basil leaves and serve as a starter.

▼ **VARIATION**

For a main course salad, add strips of cooked chicken, tuna, or diced crispy bacon.

▼ **COOK'S TIP**

- Avocados are one of the most delicious superfoods, easily digested and provide a rich source of omega fats, plus anti-oxidants vitamins A, C and E.

- Ripen at room temperature: they are ready when the flesh just yields to gentle pressure. Once ripe, they should be eaten as soon as possible.

Warm chicken liver salad

Serves 4

Hands-on time: 20 minutes

Cooking time: 8–10 minutes

280 cals, 19g fat (of which 5g saturates), 3g carbohydrate per serving

450g (1lb) chicken livers

1–2 tbsp balsamic vinegar

1 level tsp Dijon mustard

2-3 tbsp olive oil

50g (2oz) streaky bacon rashers, de-rinded
and cut into small, neat pieces (lardons)

$^1/_2$ curly endive, about 175g (6oz)

100g (3$^1/_2$oz) rocket

1 bunch spring onions, sliced

1 Drain the chicken livers on kitchen paper, then trim and cut into pieces.

2 To make the dressing for the salad, put the balsamic vinegar, mustard, 4 tbsp of the oil, and salt and pepper into a small bowl. Whisk together and set aside.

3 In a non-stick frying pan, fry the lardons until beginning to brown, stirring from time to time. Add the remaining oil and the chicken livers and stir-fry over a high heat for 2–3 minutes or until just pink in the centre.

4 Meanwhile, toss the endive, rocket and spring onions with the dressing in a large bowl. Divide between 4 plates. Arrange the warm livers and bacon on top. Serve at once, with strips of sun dried tomatoes or roasted red pepper on the side.

Spinach, pea and feta cheese salad

Serves 4

Hands-on time: 10 minutes

Cooking time: 5 minutes

180 cals, 12g fat (of which 6g saturates), 6g carbohydrate per serving

200g (7oz) each petits pois and baby leaf spinach

20g (³/₄oz) mint

200g (7oz) feta cheese

¹/₂ lemon

1 tbsp olive oil

1 Cook the petits pois according to the packet instructions. Drain and allow to cool.

2 Put the baby leaf spinach in a large bowl. Roughly chop the mint leaves and add to the bowl along with the cooled peas. Crumble the feta cheese over the top and roughly toss the salad together.

3 To make the dressing, put the lemon juice in a small bowl. Add the olive oil and whisk together well. Season to taste with freshly ground black pepper and a little salt, then, just before serving, drizzle it over the salad and toss briefly.

Spinach and carrot salad

Serves 4

Hands-on time: 15 minutes

Cooking time: 2 minutes

190 cals, 14g fat (of which 2g saturates), 10g carbohydrate per serving

350g (12oz) carrots

225g (8oz) French beans

350g (12oz) baby leaf spinach

1 garlic clove

2 tsp each soy sauce and honey

1 tbsp cider vinegar

4 tbsp olive oil

1 Slice the carrots and trim the beans. Cook the carrots in salted, boiling water for 3–4 minutes, adding the French beans for the last minute. Drain and rinse in cold water. Put both in a bowl with the spinach.

2 Crush the garlic clove and put in a small bowl. Add the soy sauce, honey, cider vinegar and olive oil. Season to taste with freshly ground black pepper and whisk together thoroughly. Pour the dressing over the carrot, bean and spinach mixture, toss together well and serve.

Easy suppers

The recipes in this chapter are designed to be appetising and comforting. They are ideal when you come home after a long day and need a satisfying meal without too much fuss or when you need to feed a hungry family.

Mixed mushroom frittata

Squash and tomato gratin

Tomato and artichoke pasta

Rocket pesto pasta

Pappardelle with spinach

Tomato risotto

Prawn, courgette and leek risotto

Lentil casserole

Chickpea stew

Chicken with fennel and tarragon

Roast cod with herb crust

Salmon and bulgur wheat pilaf

Crusted trout

Grilled lemon and thyme mackerel

Sesame beef

Healthy burgers

Mediterranean chicken

Pork with basil, tomato and stilton

Lamb steaks with mixed bean salad

Mixed mushroom frittata

Serves 4

Hands-on time: 15 minutes

Cooking time: 15–20 minutes

180 cals, 14g fat (of which 3g saturates), 0g carbohydrate per serving

1 tbsp olive oil

300g (11oz) mixed mushrooms, sliced

2 tbsp chopped thyme

Zest and juice of $1/2$ organic lemon

6 medium eggs

50g (2oz) watercress, chopped

1 Heat the oil in a large deep frying pan over a medium heat. Add the mushrooms and thyme and stir-fry for 4–5 minutes until starting to soften and brown. Stir in the lemon zest and juice, then let bubble for 1 minute. Reduce the heat.

2 Preheat the grill. Break the eggs into a bowl and beat. Add the watercress, season with salt and pepper and pour into the pan. Cook on the hob for 7–8 minutes until the sides and base are firm but the centre is still a little soft.

3 Transfer the pan to the grill and cook for 4–5 minutes until just set. Cut the frittata into quarters to serve.

▼ SERVE WITH

Stoneground, wholegrain bread and a crisp green salad.

▼ COOK'S TIP

Watercress is a superfood. It had valuable health-enhancing properties and is a good source of iron and vitamins C and E. Eat it as often as you like. Add to salads, sandwiches, grilled meat and fish dishes. Finely chopped watercress can be stirred into soups, giving them a fresh peppery tang

Squash and tomato gratin

Serves 4–6

Hands-on time: 20 minutes

Cooking time: 50 minutes – 1 hour

180–120 cals, 9–6g fat (of which 6–4g saturates), 23–16g carbohydrate per serving

1kg (2lb) piece of orange-fleshed winter
   squash (such as kabocha)
450g (1lb) ripe tomatoes
2 celery sticks or tops of small whole head
40g (1$\frac{1}{2}$oz) butter
Garlic, (optional)
A little chopped parsley, plus a sprig to garnish
About 4 tbsp coarse sourdough or wholewheat
   breadcrumbs

1 Preheat the oven to 180°C (160°C fan oven) mark 4. Peel the squash, discard the seeds and the cottony centre core, then cut into small chunks. Chop the tomatoes. Wash and chop the celery.

2 Heat 25g (1oz) of the butter in a large frying pan with a heavy base, add the celery and squash and cook gently, uncovered, until the squash is soft and just beginning to look slightly jammy. Transfer it to a shallow gratin dish.

3 In the same pan, cook the tomatoes with the garlic if using, and the chopped parsley. When most of the moisture has evaporated and the tomatoes are almost in a purée, mix with the squash, and check the seasoning. Smooth down the top (the dish should be quite full).

4 Cover with the breadcrumbs and the remaining butter cut into tiny knobs, then stand the gratin dish on a baking sheet and cook near the top of the oven for 35–40 minutes until the top is golden and crisp. Garnish with a sprig of parsley before serving.

Tomato and artichoke pasta

Serves 4

Hands-on time: 10 minutes

Cooking time: 10–12 minutes

360 cals, 7g fat (of which 3g saturates), 61g carbohydrate per serving

300g (11oz) penne

6 pieces sunblush tomatoes in oil

1 red onion, sliced

About 10 pieces roasted artichoke hearts in oil

50g (2oz) pitted black olives

50g (2oz) pecorino cheese

100g (3^1/$_2$oz) rocket

1 Cook the pasta in a pan of boiling water according to the packet instructions; keep it *al dente*. Drain well.

2 Meanwhile, drain the sunblush tomatoes, reserving the oil, and roughly chop. Heat 1 tbsp oil from the tomatoes in a large frying pan, add the onion and fry for 5–6 minutes until softened and turning golden. Drain the artichokes and roughly chop with the olives. Add to the pan with the tomatoes and heat for 3–4 minutes until hot.

3 Grate in half the pecorino cheese and stir through. Remove from the heat and stir in the rocket and pasta. Divide the pasta among four bowls and grate the remaining pecorino over the top to serve.

Rocket pesto pasta

Serves 6
Hands-on time: 5 minutes
Cooking time: 10 minutes
440 cals, 21g fat (of which 4g saturates), 53g carbohydrate per serving

425g (15oz) dried pasta

75g (3oz) goat's cheese or low-fat soft cheese

25g (1oz) grated Gruyère or Emmental cheese

100ml (4fl oz) olive oil

25g (1oz) shelled unsalted pistachio nuts

1 fresh garlic clove

75g (3oz) rocket leaves

1 Cook the pasta in a large pan of boiling water according to the packet instructions; keep it *al dente*.

2 Meanwhile, blend all the remaining ingredients in a food processor to form a smooth pesto. Drain the pasta, tip back into the pan and add the pesto. If the sauce seems too thick loosen with $^1/_2$ tbsps of hot water. Toss well and serve.

▼ **COOK'S TIP**

- Raw garlic is renowned for its curative and protective powers, which include lowering blood pressure and cholesterol levels.

- Fresh garlic has juicy, mild cloves and is available from May throughout the summer. It is the classic form of garlic to use to make e.g. pesto, salsa verde, garlic mayonnaise and chilled soups. It is usually far more digestible than dried garlic and is the best garlic to eat raw.

Pappardelle with spinach

Serves 4
Hands-on time: 10 minutes
Cooking time: 10–12 minutes
410 cals, 11g fat (of which 2g saturates), 67g carbohydrate per serving

350g (12oz) pappardelle

350g (12oz) baby leaf spinach

2 tbsp olive oil

75g (3oz) ricotta

Freshly grated nutmeg

1 Cook the pappardelle in a large pan of boiling water according to the packet instructions.

2 Meanwhile, roughly chop the spinach. Drain the pasta well, return to the pan and add the spinach, oil and ricotta, tossing for 10–15 seconds or until the spinach has wilted. Season with salt and pepper and a little freshly grated nutmeg and serve immediately.

Tomato risotto

Serves 6
Hands-on time: 10 minutes
Cooking time: about 25 minutes
270 cals, 5g fat (of which 1g saturates), 50g carbohydrate per serving

1 small onion

300g (11oz) cherry tomatoes

1 large rosemary sprig

2 tbsp olive oil

350g (12oz) risotto rice, such as arborio

4 tbsp dry white wine

750ml (1$\frac{1}{4}$ pints) hot vegetable stock

Shavings of Parmesan to serve

1 Finely chop the onion and halve the cherry tomatoes. Pull the leaves from the rosemary and chop roughly. Set aside.

2 Heat the oil in a flameproof casserole, add the onion and cook for about 8–10 minutes or until beginning to soften. Add the rice and stir to coat in the oil and onion. Pour in the wine, then the hot stock, stirring well to mix.

3 Bring to the boil, stirring, then cover and simmer for 5 minutes. Stir in the tomatoes and chopped rosemary. Simmer, covered, for a further 10–15 minutes or until the rice is tender and most of the liquid has been absorbed. Season to taste.

4 Serve immediately with shavings of Parmesan, a large green salad and extra virgin olive oil to drizzle over.

Prawn, courgette and leek risotto

Serves 4-6

Hands-on time: 10 minutes

Cooking time: 30 minutes

460–310 cals, 10–6g fat (of which 3g saturates), 72–48g carbohydrate per serving

1 tbsp olive oil

25g (1oz) butter

1 leek, finely chopped

2 courgettes, finely chopped

2 garlic cloves, crushed

350g (12oz) arborio risotto rice

100ml ($3^1/_2$fl oz) dry white wine

1.5 litres ($2^3/_4$ pints) hot, vegetable stock

200g (7oz) cooked Icelandic prawns

Small bunch parsley or mint, or a mixture of both

1 In a large, shallow pan, heat the oil and half the butter, then add the leek, courgettes and garlic and soften over a low heat. Add the rice and stir well, so it soaks up the melted butter, and cook for 1 minute before pouring in the wine. Let bubble until the wine has evaporated.

2 Meanwhile, in another large pan, heat the stock to a low, steady simmer. Ladle the stock into the risotto slowly, adding the next ladleful only when all the stock has been absorbed. Stir constantly to ensure that the risotto is creamy.

3 When nearly all the stock has been added, add the cooked prawns. Season to taste and stir in the remaining stock and the rest of the butter. Stir through and take off the heat. Cover and leave to stand for a couple of minutes before stirring the chopped herbs through and serving.

4 Serve immediately with a green salad or cooked french beans.

Lentil casserole

Serves 6
Hands-on time: 20 minutes
Cooking time: about 1 hour
220 cals, 6g fat (of which 1g saturates), 32g carbohydrate per serving

2 tbsp olive oil

2 medium onions, sliced

4 medium carrots, sliced

3 medium leeks, sliced

450g (1lb) button mushrooms

2 garlic cloves, crushed

2.5cm (1in) piece fresh root ginger, grated

1 tbsp ground coriander

225g (8oz) split red lentils

750ml (1¼ pints) hot vegetable stock

4 tbsp chopped coriander

1 Preheat the oven to 180°C (160°C fan oven) mark 4. Heat the oil in a flameproof, ovenproof casserole, add the onions, carrots and leeks and fry, stirring, for 5 minutes. Add the mushrooms, garlic, ginger and ground coriander, and fry for 2–3 minutes.

2 Rinse and drain the lentils, then stir into the casserole with the stock. Season with salt and pepper and return to the boil. Cover and cook in the oven for 45–50 minutes until the vegetables and lentils are tender. Stir in the chopped coriander before serving.

Chickpea stew

Serves 4
Hands-on time: 10 minutes
Cooking time: about 35 minutes
170 cals, 7g fat (of which 1g saturates), 20g carbohydrate per serving

1 tbsp olive oil

1 onion, finely chopped

2 garlic cloves, sliced

1 tbsp harissa

2 tbsp tomato purée

$\frac{1}{2}$ tsp ground cumin

1 aubergine, chopped

1 each red, green and yellow pepper, halved,
   deseeded and chopped

400g (16oz) canned chickpeas, drained

450ml ($\frac{3}{4}$ pint) hot vegetable stock

1 Heat the oil in a pan, add the onion and fry for 5–10 minutes until softened. Add the garlic, harissa, tomato purée and cumin. Cook, stirring, for 2 minutes.

2 Add the aubergine and peppers, stir everything together, and cook for 2 minutes. Add the chickpeas and stock. Season with salt and pepper, then bring to the boil. Simmer for 20 minutes, then serve.

▼ **SERVE WITH**

50g (2oz) bulgur wheat per person, cooked according to the packet instructions.

Chicken with fennel and tarragon

Serves 4
Hands-on time: 10 minutes
Cooking time: 45–55 minutes
280 cals, 22g fat (of which 9g saturates), 6g carbohydrate per serving

1 tbsp olive oil

4 chicken thighs

1 onion

1 fennel bulb

$^1/_2$ lemon

200ml (7fl oz) hot chicken stock

200g tub half-fat crème fraîche

1 small bunch tarragon

1 Preheat the oven to 200°C (180°C fan) mark 6. Heat the olive oil in a large flameproof casserole. Add the chicken thighs and fry for 5 minutes until brown, then remove and set them aside to keep warm.

2 Finely chop the onion and slice the fennel. Add the onion to the pan and fry for 5 minutes, then add the fennel and cook for 5–10 minutes until softened.

3 Squeeze the juice from the lemon and pour into the pan, then add the stock. Bring to a simmer and cook until sauce is reduced by half.

4 Stir in the crème fraîche and return the chicken to the pan. Stir once to mix, then cover and cook in the oven for 25–30 minutes. Roughly chop the tarragon and stir it into the sauce. Serve with basmati or wild rice.

Roast cod with herb crust

Serves 4

Hands-on time: 5 minutes

Cooking time: 15–20 minutes

230 cals, 11g fat (of which 1g saturates), 9g carbohydrate per serving

4 tbsp each chopped parsley and coriander

Zest of 1 organic lemon

2 tbsp olive oil

25g (1oz) ground almonds

2 slices wholemeal bread with crusts removed,
  torn into rough chunks

4 x 125g (4oz) cod fillets

1 Preheat the oven to 200°C (180°C fan oven) mark 6. Put all the ingredients except the cod into a food processor and whiz until finely chopped.

2 Put the cod in a baking dish. Spread the breadcrumb mixture on top of each piece of fish. Roast for 15–20 minutes until the cod is cooked. Serve with sweet potatoes and green vegetables.

Salmon and bulgur wheat pilaf

Serves 4
Hands-on time: 5 minutes
Cooking time: 20 minutes
400 cals, 13g fat (of which 3g saturates), 43g carbohydrate per serving

1 tbsp olive oil

1 onion, chopped

175g (6oz) bulgur wheat

450ml (12fl oz) vegetable stock

400g (14oz) canned pink salmon, drained
  and flaked

125g (4oz) spinach

225g (8oz) frozen peas

Juice and zest of 1 organic lemon

1 Heat the oil in a large saucepan, add the onion and cook until softened. Stir in the bulgur wheat to coat with the oil, then stir in the stock and bring to the boil. Cover, reduce the heat and simmer for 10–15 minutes until the stock has been fully absorbed.

2 Stir in the salmon, spinach, peas and lemon juice and cook until the spinach has wilted and the salmon and peas are heated through. Season and sprinkle with lemon zest before serving.

Crusted trout

Serves 4
Hands-on time: 10 minutes
Cooking time: 10–13 minutes
280 cals, 14g fat (of which 5g saturates), 1g carbohydrate per serving

1 tbsp sesame oil

1 tbsp soy sauce

Juice of 1 lime

4 x 150g (5oz) trout fillets

2 tbsp sesame seeds

1 Preheat the grill. Put the sesame oil in a bowl. Add the soy sauce and lime juice and whisk together.

2 Put the trout fillets on a baking sheet, pour the sesame mixture over them and grill for 8–10 minutes. Sprinkle with the sesame seeds and grill for a further 2–3 minutes until the seeds are golden. Serve with a lime wedge, a herb salad and some finely sliced fennel.

▼ **COOK'S TIP**

Sesame seeds are deliciously nutty and highly nutritious. They are a valuable source of protein, good omega fats and vitamin E. Lightly toasted sesame seeds, crushed with a little salt and stirred into 1–2 tbsp of olive oil, make an excellant salad dressing for cooked green beans, broccoli and carrots.

Grilled lemon and thyme mackerel

Serves 4

Hands-on time: 10 minutes

Cooking time: 5–6 minutes

360 cals, 28g fat (of which 6g saturates), 0g carbohydrate per serving

4 whole mackerel, heads removed, gutted

  (ask your fishmonger to do this for you)

1 organic lemon

4 lemon thyme sprigs

2 tbsp olive oil

1 Preheat the grill to high. Put the mackerel on a large baking sheet and cut three slashes in the side of each one.

2 Grate the zest of the lemon and finely chop the lemon thyme sprigs, then sprinkle both over the fish. Drizzle with the oil, season and squeeze the juice from half of the lemon over the top.

3 Put the mackerel under the grill for 5–6 minutes until cooked through. Serve with bulgur, a green salad and lemon wedges.

▼ **COOK'S TIP**

Oily fish such as mackerel, herring and sardines are one of the best sources of essential heart-protecting omega-3 oils. Eat them at least once a week. Fresh Cornish mackerel are a treat and inexpensive – look out for them in your fishmonger's and fresh fish counters at supermarkets.

Sesame beef

Serves 4

Hands-on time: 20 minutes

Cooking time: about 10 minutes

200 cals, 10g fat (of which 3g saturates), 5g carbohydrate per serving

2 tbsp each soy sauce and Worcestershire sauce

2 level tsp tomato purée

Juice of $\frac{1}{2}$ lemon

1 tbsp sesame seeds

1 garlic clove, crushed

400g (14oz) rump steak, sliced

1 tbsp vegetable oil

3 small pak choi, chopped

1 bunch spring onions, sliced

1 In a bowl, mix together the soy, Worcestershire sauce, tomato purée, lemon juice, sesame seeds and garlic. Add the steak and toss to coat.

2 Heat the oil in a large wok or non-stick frying pan until hot. Add the steak and sear well. Remove from the wok and set aside.

3 Add any sauce from the bowl to the wok and heat for 1 minute. Add the pak choi, spring onions and steak, and stir-fry for 5 minutes.

▼ **SERVE WITH**

Fresh egg pasta e.g. fettucine, tagliatelli. Use 50g (2oz) per person, cooked according to the packet instructions. Toss with the beef stir-fry before serving.

Healthy burgers

Serves 4
Hands-on time: 10 minutes
Cooking time: 6–12 minutes
80 cals, 1g fat (of which trace saturates), 13g carbohydrate per serving

450g (1lb) top-quality lean minced beef

1 onion, very finely chopped

1 tbsp Herbes de Provence

2 tsp sun-dried tomato paste

1 medium egg, beaten

1 In a bowl, mix together the minced beef, onion, herbs, sun-dried tomato paste and beaten egg. Season with pepper, then shape the mixture into four round burgers about 2cm ($^3/_4$in) thick.

2 Preheat the grill or griddle pan. Cook the burgers for 4–6 minutes on each side.

▼ **SERVE WITH**

Chilli coleslaw: put 3 peeled and finely shredded carrots in a large bowl. Add $^1/_2$ finely shredded white cabbage, 1 finely sliced, deseeded red pepper and $^1/_2$ chopped cucumber. In a small bowl, mix together $^1/_2$ tsp harissa, 100g ($3^1/_2$oz) natural yogurt and 1 tbsp white wine vinegar. Add to the vegetables and toss well. Serves 4 as an accompaniment.

Mediterranean chicken

Serves 4

Hands-on time: 15 minutes

Cooking time: 45 minutes

250 cals, 12g fat (of which 3g saturates), 7g carbohydrate per serving

1 tbsp olive oil

1 onion, finely chopped

2 garlic cloves, finely chopped

4 x 125g (4oz) skinless chicken breasts

2 courgettes, roughly chopped

400g (14oz) canned chopped tomatoes

100g ($3^1/_2$ oz) olives, roughly chopped

2tbsp capers

4tbsp roughly chopped basil

1 Heat the oil in a non-stick flameproof casserole. Add the onion; cook for 7–8 minutes until soft. Add the garlic; cook for 1 minute.

2 Add the chicken to the casserole and cook for 5 minutes. Add the courgette, tomatoes, olives, capers and basil, then cover and cook for 30 minutes over a low heat until the chicken is cooked through.

Pork with basil, tomato and stilton

Serves 4
Hands-on time: 10 minutes
Cooking time: 10–14 minutes
230 cals, 13g fat (of which 6g saturates), 1g carbohydrate per serving

4 pork loin steaks

1 ripe beef tomato, sliced

Few basil leaves

50g (2oz) Stilton cheese, sliced

1 Preheat the grill. Grill the pork for 4–5 minutes on each side.

2 Divide the sliced tomato among the steaks, with a few basil leaves and the sliced Stilton, and grill for a further 1–2 minutes until the cheese has melted and the pork is cooked through. Serve with new potatoes and runner beans.

Lamb steaks with mixed bean salad

Serves 4

Hands-on time: 5 minutes

Cooking time: about 10 minutes

450 cals, 23g fat (of which 9g saturates), 19g carbohydrate per serving

150g (5oz) sunblush tomatoes in oil

1 garlic clove, crushed

Few rosemary sprigs

4 x 175g (6oz) leg of lamb steaks

$^1/_2$ small red onion, finely sliced

2 x 400g (14oz) cans mixed beans, drained
  and rinsed

Large handful of rocket

1 Preheat the grill to high. Drain the sunblush tomatoes, reserving the oil. Put the garlic in a large, shallow dish with 1 tbsp oil from the tomatoes. Snip the rosemary leaves into small pieces and add half to the dish. Season with salt and pepper, then add the lamb and toss to coat.

2 Grill the lamb for 3–4 minutes on each side until cooked but still just pink. Roughly chop the tomatoes and put into a pan with the onion, beans, remaining rosemary, rocket and a further 1 tbsp oil from the tomatoes. Warm through until the rocket starts to wilt. Serve the lamb steaks with the salad on warmed plates.

Food for friends

Cooking and sharing a meal with friends is one of life's great pleasures. Low-GI entertaining is no exception. Whether you need recipes for special occasions, weekends or informal gatherings, this section is packed with ideas.

Falafel

Makes about 24
Hands-on time: 20–25 minutes, plus overnight soaking and standing time
Cooking time: 8–10 minutes
70 cals, 5g fat (of which 1g saturates), 5g carbohydrate per serving

225g (8oz) dried chickpeas, soaked overnight

1 tbsp tahini paste

1 garlic clove, crushed

1 tsp sea salt

1 tsp ground turmeric

1 tsp ground cumin

$^1/_4$ tsp cayenne pepper

2 tbsp chopped coriander

1 tbsp chopped mint

1 tbsp lemon juice

Seasoned flour, to dust

Oil, to shallow-fry

1 Drain the soaked chickpeas. Put into a food processor and process to a fairly smooth paste.

2 Transfer to a bowl and add the tahini paste, garlic, salt, spices, herbs and lemon juice. Stir well, then cover and leave to stand for at least 30 minutes to allow the flavours to develop.

3 With floured hands, shape the chickpea mixture into 2.5cm (1in) balls. Flatten slightly and dust with the seasoned flour.

4 Heat a 1cm ($^1/_2$ in) depth of oil in a frying pan. When hot, fry the balls in batches for 1–2 minutes on each side until evenly browned. Drain on crumpled kitchen paper and keep warm while cooking the rest.

5 Serve the falafel warm or cool, with a greek style yogurt, flavoured with a crushed clove of garlic and chopped mint, and some warm pitta bread.

Italian sausage stew

Serves 4
Hands-on time: 10 minutes, plus soaking time
Cooking time: 15 minutes
400 cals, 30g fat (of which 103g saturates), 11g carbohydrate per serving

25g (1oz) dried porcini mushrooms

300g (11oz) whole rustic Italian salami

  sausages, such as salami Milano

2 tbsp olive oil

1 onion, sliced

2 garlic cloves, chopped

1 small red chilli, deseeded and chopped

1 tender rosemary stem, plus sprigs

  to garnish

400g (14oz) canned chopped tomatoes

200ml (7fl oz) red wine

1 Put the dried mushrooms in a small bowl, pour on 100ml ($3^{1}/_{2}$fl oz) boiling water and leave to soak for 20 minutes or soften in the microwave on high for $3^{1}/_{2}$ minutes and leave to cool. Cut the salami into 1cm ($^{1}/_{2}$in) slices and set aside.

2 Heat the olive oil in a pan, add the onion, garlic and chilli and fry gently for 5 minutes. Meanwhile, strip the leaves from the rosemary stem and add them to the pan, stirring.

3 Add the salami and fry for 2 minutes on each side or until browned. Drain and chop the mushrooms and add them to the pan. Stir in the chopped tomatoes and red wine, then season with pepper. Simmer, uncovered, for 5 minutes. Serve with pasta or grilled polenta.

Baked tomatoes and fennel

Serves 6

Hands-on time: 10 minutes

Cooking time: 1 hour 15 minutes

140 cals, 12g fat (of which 2g saturates), 7g carbohydrate per serving

900g (2lb) fennel, trimmed and cut into quarters

75ml ($2^1/_2$ fl oz) white wine

5 thyme sprigs

75ml ($2^1/_2$ fl oz) olive oil

900g (2lb) ripe beef or plum tomatoes

1 Preheat the oven to 200°C (180°C fan oven) mark 6. Put the fennel in a roasting tin and pour the white wine over it. Snip the thyme sprigs over the fennel and drizzle with the oil.

2 Roast for 45 minutes. Halve the tomatoes, add to the roasting tin and continue to roast for 30 minutes or until tender, basting with the juices halfway through.

▼ **COOK'S TIP**

This dish is an ideal accompaniment to grilled fish or meat, or a vegetarian frittata.

Lentil, orange and ginger stew

Serves 4

Hands-on time: 15 minutes

Cooking time: 26–28 minutes

310 cals, 9g fat (of which 1g saturates), 42g carbohydrate per serving

1 tbsp olive oil

1 leek, diced

2 carrots, diced

250g (9oz) Puy lentils

1.5 litres (2$^1/_2$ pints) hot vegetable stock

200g (7oz) cherry tomatoes on the vine

2 organic oranges

2.5cm (1in) piece fresh root ginger,

   grated

25g (1oz) almonds, roughly chopped

100g (3$^1/_2$oz) spinach leaves

1 Preheat the oven to 200°C (180°C fan oven) mark 6. Heat 2 tsp oil in an ovenproof pan, add the leek and carrots and fry for 6–8 minutes. Stir in the lentils, coating them with the mixture, then pour in the stock. Season to taste, cover and bring to the boil, then reduce the heat. Transfer to the oven for 20 minutes or until lentils are just tender with a slight bite.

2 After the lentils have been cooking for 10 minutes, put the tomatoes into a roasting tin, drizzle with the remaining oil and roast for 8–10 minutes.

3 Meanwhile, remove the skin from the oranges with a sharp knife and cut the oranges into slices, reserving any juice. When the lentils are cooked, add the orange slices, juice and the remaining ingredients. Spoon into bowls with the tomatoes.

Spicy bean and tomato fajitas

Serves 6

Hands-on time: 15 minutes

cooking time: 23 minutes

460 cals, 23g fat, (of which 5g saturates) 51g carbohydrate per serving

2 tbsp sunflower oil

1 medium onion, sliced

2 garlic cloves, crushed

$1/2$ tsp hot chilli powder

1 tsp ground coriander

1 tsp ground cumin

1 tbsp tomato purée

400g (14oz) canned chopped tomatoes

225g (8oz) canned red kidney beans, drained and rinsed

300g (11oz) canned borlotti beans, drained and rinsed

300g (11oz) canned flageolet beans, drained and rinsed

150ml ($1/4$ pint) hot vegetable stock

2 ripe avocados, quartered and chopped

Juice of $1/2$ lime

1 tbsp chopped coriander, plus sprigs to garnish

6 ready-made flour tortillas

145ml ($4^1/2$ fl oz) soured cream

Lime wedges, to serve

1 Heat the oil in a large pan, add the onion and cook gently for 5 minutes. Add the garlic and spices and cook for a further 2 minutes.

2 Add the tomato purée and cook for 1 minute, then add the tomatoes, beans and hot stock. Season well with salt and pepper, bring to the boil and simmer for 15 minutes, stirring occasionally.

3 Put the avocado into a bowl, add the lime juice and the chopped coriander and mash together. Season to taste.

4 Warm the tortillas: either wrap them in foil and heat in the oven at 180°C (160°C fan oven) mark 4 for 10 minutes or put on a plate and microwave on high for 45 seconds.

5 Spoon the beans down the centre of each tortilla. Fold up one edge to keep the filling inside, then wrap the two sides in so they overlap. Spoon on the avocado and top with soured cream. Garnish with coriander sprigs and serve with lime wedges.

Spinach and goat's cheese frittata

Serves 4

Hands-on time: 20 minutes

Cooking time: 12 minutes

260 cals, 19g fat (of which 7g saturates), 3g carbohydrate per serving

200g (7oz) baby leeks

4 spring onions

125g (4oz) baby leaf spinach

6 large eggs

4 tbsp milk

Freshly grated nutmeg

125g (4oz) soft goat's cheese

1 tbsp olive oil

1 Preheat the grill to high. Chop the leeks and spring onions. Blanch the leeks in a pan of salted boiling water for 2 minutes. Add the spinach and spring onions just before the end. Drain, rinse in cold water and dry on kitchen paper.

2 In a bowl, whisk together the eggs, milk and nutmeg. Season with salt and pepper. Chop the goat's cheese and then stir it into the egg mixture with the leeks, spinach and spring onions.

3 Heat the oil in a non-stick frying pan. Pour in the frittata mixture and fry gently for 4–5 minutes, then finish under the hot grill for 4–5 minutes until the top is golden and just firm.

Spicy swordfish

Serves 4

Hands-on time: 15 minutes

Cooking time: 10–13 minutes

130 cals, 4g fat (of which 1g saturates), 1g carbohydrate per serving

2 red chillies, deseeded and finely chopped

  (see page 49)

2 tbsp chopped mint or coriander

3 tbsp sherry vinegar

1 tbsp olive oil

4 x 125g (4oz) swordfish steaks

8 spring onions, halved

Lime wedges, to serve

1 In a large, shallow dish, mix together the chillies, mint or coriander, sherry vinegar and oil. Add the swordfish steaks and coat in the dressing.

2 Preheat a griddle pan. Remove the fish from the dressing and cook, in batches, on each side for about 4–5 minutes. Transfer to plates. Add the spring onions to the griddle pan with the remaining dressing and cook for 2–3 minutes. Top the fish with the spring onions, drizzle with the juices and serve with lime wedges to squeeze over the fish.

▼ SERVE WITH

Cherry tomatoes, grilled for 5–10 minutes until just soft. Also serve with 50g (2oz) bulgur wheat per person, cooked according to the packet instructions. Stir through 2 tbsp chopped parsley before serving.

Seafood spaghetti with pepper and almond sauce

Serves 4

Hands-on time: 20 minutes

Cooking time: 25 minutes

290 cals, 9g fat (of which 1g saturates), 28g carbohydrate per serving

1 small red pepper

1 red chilli (see page 49)

50g (2oz) blanched almonds

2–3 garlic cloves

2 tbsp red wine vinegar

350ml (12fl oz) tomato juice

Small handful of flat-leaved parsley

300g (11oz) spaghetti

450g (1lb) mixed, cooked seafood, such as

   Icelandic prawns, mussels and squid

1 Preheat the grill. Put the pepper and chilli under the grill and cook, turning occasionally, until the skins char and blacken. Cool slightly, then peel off the skins. Halve, discard seeds, then put the flesh into a food processor.

2 Toast the almonds under the grill until golden. Chop the garlic. Add the toasted almonds and garlic to the processor with the red wine vinegar, tomato juice and half the parsley, then season with salt and pepper. Blend until almost smooth, then transfer to a large pan.

3 Meanwhile, cook the spaghetti in a pan of boiling water according to the packet instructions; keep it *al dente*. Heat the sauce gently until it simmers, then add the seafood. Simmer for 3–4 minutes or until the sauce and seafood have heated through, stirring frequently. Roughly chop the remaining parsley. Drain the pasta, return to the pan, then add the sauce together with the parsley and toss well.

Coconut fish pilau

Serves 4

Hands-on time: 15 minutes

Cooking time: about 30 minutes

430 cals, 12g fat (of which 4g saturates), 53g carbohydrate per serving

2 tsp olive oil

1 shallot, chopped

1 tbsp Thai green curry paste

225g (8oz) brown basmati rice

600ml (1 pint) hot fish or vegetable stock

150ml ($^1/_4$ pint) reduced-fat coconut milk

350g (12oz) skinless cod fillet, cut into
   bite-sized pieces

350g (12oz) sugar snap peas

125g (4oz) cooked and peeled Icelandic prawns

25g (1oz) toasted almonds, chopped

Squeeze of lemon juice

2 tbsp chopped coriander

1 Heat the oil in a frying pan, add the shallot and 1 tbsp water and fry for 4–5 minutes until golden. Stir in the curry paste and cook for 1–2 minutes.

2 Add the rice, stock and coconut milk. Bring to the boil, then cover and simmer for 15–20 minutes until all the liquid has been absorbed.

3 Add the cod and cook for 3–5 minutes. Add the sugar snap peas, prawns, almonds and lemon juice. Check the seasoning. Garnish with coriander.

Easy chicken casserole

Serves 6

Hands-on time: 15 minutes

Cooking time: 50 minutes

270 cals, 8g fat (of which 2g saturates), 17g carbohydrate per serving without chicken skin

1 rosemary sprig

2 bay leaves

1 small organic chicken

1 red onion, cut into wedges

2 carrots, cut into chunks

2 leeks, cut into chunks

2 celery sticks, cut into chunks

12 baby new potatoes

900ml (1^1/$_2$ pints) hot vegetable stock

200g (7oz) green beans, trimmed

1 Preheat the oven to 180°C (160°C fan oven) mark 4. Put the herbs and chicken in a large ovenproof and flameproof casserole. Add the onion, carrots, leeks, celery, potatoes and stock. Bring to the boil, then cook in oven for 45 minutes or until the chicken is cooked.

2 Add the beans and cook for 5 minutes. Carve the chicken and divide among six bowls. Spoon the vegetables on top and ladle the stock over it.

Orange and herb chicken

Serves 4

Hands-on time: 10 minutes

Cooking time: 30 minutes

170 cals, 7g fat (of which 2g saturates), 1g carbohydrate per serving

125ml (4fl oz) orange juice

Zest of 1 organic orange

4 small orange wedges

2 tbsp freshly chopped tarragon

2 tbsp flat-leaved parsley

1 tbsp olive oil

1 garlic clove, crushed

4 skinless chicken breasts

1 Preheat the oven to 200°C (180°C fan over) mark 6. In a large bowl, whisk together the orange juice, orange zest, herbs and garlic. Season to taste.

2 Slash the chicken breasts several times and put in an ovenproof dish. Pour the marinade over them and top each with an orange wedge.

3 Cook in the oven for 20–30 minutes or until cooked through. Serve on brown or wild rice and watercress salad.

Steak with onions and tagliatelle

Serves 4

Hands-on time: 10 minutes

Cooking time: 20 minutes

400 cals, 14g fat (of which 8g saturates), 37g carbohydrate per serving

225g (8oz) tagliatelle

2 x 200g (7oz) sirloin steaks

2 red onions

200g (7oz) low-fat crème fraîche

Small handful of flat-leaved parsley

1 Cook the pasta in a large pan of boiling water according to the packet instructions; keep it *al dente*.

2 Meanwhile, season the steaks on both sides with salt and pepper. Heat a non-stick frying pan until really hot and fry the steaks for 2–3 minutes each side until brown but still pink inside. Remove from the pan and set aside.

3 Slice the onions into thin wedges, then add to the pan and stir-fry for 8–10 minutes until softened and golden. Add a little water if they're sticking. Season, reduce the heat and stir in the crème fraîche.

4 Cut the fat off the steaks and discard, then cut the meat into thin strips. Add to the pan and cook briskly for 1–2 minutes, then stir in the pasta. Snip the parsley over it, toss again and serve immediately.

Spiced lamb with lentils

Serves 4
Hands-on time: 10 minutes
Cooking time: 2 hours
380 cals, 14g fat (of which 5g saturates), 31g carbohydrate per serving

1 tbsp sunflower oil

8 lamb chops, trimmed of all fat

2 onions, finely sliced

1 tsp each paprika and ground cinnamon

400g (14oz) canned lentils, drained

400g (14oz) canned chickpeas, drained

300ml ($\frac{1}{2}$ pint) lamb or chicken stock

1 Preheat the oven to 180°C (160° fan oven) mark 4. Heat the oil in a large, non-stick frying pan, add the chops and brown on both sides. Remove from pan with a slotted spoon.

2 Add the onions, paprika and cinnamon. Fry for 2–3 minutes. Stir in the lentils and chickpeas. Season, then spoon into a shallow 2-litre (3$\frac{1}{2}$-pint) ovenproof dish.

3 Put the chops on top of the onion and lentil mixture and pour over stock over them.

4 Cover the dish tightly and cook in the oven for 1$\frac{1}{2}$ hours or until the chops are tender. Uncover and cook for 30 minutes or until lightly browned.

Pork steaks with sage and Parma ham

Serves 4
Hands-on time: 5 minutes
Cooking time: 10 minutes
380 cals, 25g fat, (of which 12g saturates), 4g carbohydrate per serving

4 pork shoulder steaks, about 150g (5oz),
  each, halved if large

4 thin slices Parma ham or pancetta

6 sage leaves

1 tbsp oil

150ml ($^1/_4$ pint) pure unsweetened apple juice

50g (2oz) chilled butter, diced

Squeeze of lemon juice

1 Put the pork steaks on a board. Lay a slice of Parma ham or pancetta and a sage leaf on each pork steak, then secure to the meat with a wooden cocktail stick. Season with pepper.

2 Heat the oil in a large frying pan with a heavy base and fry the pork for about 3–4 minutes on each side until golden brown.

3 Pour in the apple juice, stirring and scraping up the sediment from the base of the pan. Let the liquid bubble until reduced by half. Lift the pork out on to a warmed plate.

4 Return the pan to the heat, add the butter and swirl until melted into the pan juices. Add lemon juice to taste and pour over the pork. Serve with curly kale or cabbage and sweet potatoes.

▼ **VARIATION**

Use white wine instead of apple juice.

Treats

Eating a low-GI diet does not mean denying yourself the pleasure of a sweet treat or dessert every now and then. There are lots of delicious ones to choose from; desserts based on fruit, for example, are perfect. You can also use low-GI fruit sugar (see p.16) as a substitute for cane sugar if you wish.

Fruit kebabs with spiced pear dip

Citus salad

Chocolate cinnamon sorbet

Lemon sorbet

Strawberry and black pepper granita

Baked apricots with almonds

Poached peaches and strawberries

Hot spiced fruit salad

Poached pears

Sweet toasted almonds

Roasted apples and oats with blueberries

Rhubarb and raspberry meringue

Apple and cranberry strudel

Chocolate and prune pudding

Almond macaroons

Mango and lime mousse

Banana and pecan muffins

Ginger and fruit tea bread

Clafoutis

Fruit kebabs with spiced pear dip

Makes 6 kebabs

Hands-on time: 20 minutes, plus soaking time

Cooking time: 8 minutes

130 cals, 2g fat (of which trace saturates), 27g carbohydrate per kebab including dip

for the Spiced Pear Dip

150g (5oz) ready-to-eat dried pears,
  soaked in hot water for about 30 minutes

Juice of 1 orange

1 level tsp finely chopped fresh
  root ginger

$\frac{1}{2}$ tsp vanilla extract

50ml (2fl oz) very low-fat natural yogurt

$\frac{1}{2}$ level tsp ground cinnamon,
  plus extra for dusting

1 tsp dark runny honey

25g (1oz) hazelnuts, toasted and
  roughly chopped

for the Fruit Kebabs

3 large fresh figs, each cut
  into quarters

1 large ripe mango, skin and
  stone removed, flesh cut
  into cubes

1 baby pineapple or 2 thick
  slices of pineapple, skin
  removed and flesh cut
  into cubes

1 tbsp dark runny honey

1 To make the dip, drain the pears and place in a food processor or blender with the orange juice, ginger, vanilla extract, yogurt, cinnamon and 50ml (2fl oz) water and process until smooth. Spoon the dip into a bowl. Drizzle with the honey, sprinkle with the toasted hazelnuts and dust with a little ground cinnamon. Cover and set aside in a cool place until ready to serve.

2 Preheat the grill to its highest setting. To make the kebabs, thread alternate pieces of fruit on six 20cm (8in) wooden kebab skewers, using at least two pieces of each type of fruit per skewer. Place the skewers on a foil-covered tray and cover the ends of the skewer with strips of foil to prevent them burning. Drizzle with honey and grill for about 4 minutes on each side, close to the heat, until lightly charred. Serve warm or at room temperature with the dip.

Citrus salad

Serves 4

Hands-on time: 15 minutes

Cooking time: 5 minutes

100 cals, 3g fat (of which trace saturates), 17g carbohydrate per serving

1 grapefruit

1 pink grapefruit

4 oranges

1 tbsp runny honey

25g (1oz) pumpkin or sunflower seeds

1 Cut off the top and bottom of the ordinary grapefruit, then use a sharp knife to peel away the pith. Slice into the flesh of each segment to remove the fruit, then tip into a bowl with any juice.

2 Do the same with the pink grapefruit and the oranges. Add the honey.

3 Toast the pumpkin or sunflower seeds in a dry frying pan until golden, then sprinkle them over the fruit. Spoon into bowls and serve with a dollop of yogurt.

Chocolate cinnamon sorbet

Serves 8

Hands-on time time: 5 minutes, plus chilling and freezing time

Cooking time: 15 minutes

130 cals, 1g fat (of which 1g saturates) 28g carbohydrate per serving

200g (7oz) golden granulated sugar

50g (2oz) cocoa powder

1 tsp instant espresso coffee powder

1 cinnamon stick

8 tsp crème de cacao (chocolate liqueur) to serve

1 Put the sugar, cocoa powder, coffee and cinnamon stick into a large pan with 600ml (1 pint) water. Bring to the boil, stirring until the sugar has completely dissolved. Boil for 5 minutes, then remove from the heat. Leave to cool. Remove the cinnamon stick, then chill.

2 If you have an ice-cream maker, put the mixture into it and churn for about 30 minutes until firm. Otherwise, pour into a freezer-proof container and put in the coldest part of the freezer until firmly frozen, then transfer the frozen mixture to a blender or food processor and blend until smooth. Quickly put the mixture back in the container and return it to the freezer for at least 1 hour.

3 To serve, scoop the sorbet into individual cups and drizzle 1 tsp chocolate liqueur over each portion. Serve immediately.

Lemon sorbet

Serves 3–4

Hands-on time: 10 minutes, plus chilling and freezing time

Cooking time: none

170–130 cals, 0g fat, 45–34g carbohydrate per serving

3 juicy organic lemons

125g (4oz) golden caster sugar

1 large egg white

1 Finely pare the lemon zest, using a zester, then squeeze the juice. Put the zest into a pan with the sugar and 350ml (12fl oz) water and heat gently to dissolve. Increase the heat and boil for 10 minutes. Leave to cool.

2 Stir the lemon juice into the cooled sugar syrup. Cover and chill in the fridge for 30 minutes.

3 Strain the syrup through a fine sieve into a bowl. In another bowl, beat the egg white until just frothy, then whisk into the lemon mixture.

4 For best results, freeze in an ice-cream maker. Otherwise, pour into a shallow freezerproof container and freeze until almost frozen; mash well with a fork and freeze until solid. Transfer the sorbet to the fridge 30 minutes before serving to soften slightly.

Strawberry and black pepper granita

Serves 6

Hands-on time: 10 minutes, plus freezing time

Cooking time: none

100 cals, 0g fat, 27g carbohydrate per serving

400g (14oz) hulled strawberries

75g (3oz) golden caster sugar

Juice of $^1/_2$ lemon

1 Put the strawberries into a food processor and whiz a purée. Add the sugar, lemon juice, a good grind of pepper and 450ml ($^3/_4$ pint) water. Pulse to mix, then pour into a freezer-proof container. Freeze for 2 hours.

2 Use a fork to stir in the frozen edges and freeze again for 1 hour. Fork through, then freeze for a further hour or overnight. Use a fork to break up the granita, then serve in tall glasses.

Baked apricots with almonds

Serves 6
Hands-on time: 10 minutes
Cooking time: 20–25 minutes
130 cals, 6g fat (of which 2g saturates), 16g carbohydrate per serving

12 apricots, halved and stoned

3 tbsp golden caster sugar

2 tbsp amaretto liqueur

25g (1oz) unsalted butter

25g (1oz) flaked almonds

1 Preheat the oven to 200°C (180°C fan oven) mark 6. Put the apricot halves, cut-side up, in an ovenproof dish. Sprinkle with the sugar, drizzle with the liqueur, then dot each apricot half with a little butter. Scatter the flaked almonds over them.

2 Bake in the oven for 20–25 minutes until the apricots are soft and the juices are syrupy. Serve warm, with crème fraîche.

Poached peaches and strawberries

Serves 4
Hands-on time: 15 minutes, plus chilling time
Cooking time: 10 minutes, plus cooling time
70 cals, 0g fat, 17g carbohydrate per serving

4 ripe peaches, halved, stoned and quartered

250ml (8fl oz) orange juice

$^1/_2$ tbsp golden caster sugar

Small pinch of ground cinnamon

225g (8oz) halved strawberries

1 Put the peaches in a pan with the orange juice, sugar and cinnamon. Simmer gently for 5 minutes. Remove the peaches with a slotted spoon and put in a bowl.

2 Let the juice bubble until reduced by half. Pour over the peaches, then cool, cover and chill. Remove from the fridge about 2 hours before serving and stir in the halved strawberries.

Hot spiced fruit salad

Serves 6

Hands-on time: 10 minutes

Cooking time: 1 hour 30 minutes

180 cals, 3g fat (trace saturates), 38g carbohydrate per serving

3 apples

3 pears

12 each ready-to-eat dried apricots and figs

Juice of 2 large oranges

150ml ($^1/_4$ pint) apple juice

A pinch of ground cinnamon

1 star anise

1 Preheat the oven to 180°C (160°C fan oven) mark 4. Core the apples and pears and chop. Put into a roasting tin with the apricots and figs, the orange juice, apple juice, ground cinnamon and star anise. Stir, cover with foil and cook in the oven for 1 hour.

2 Remove the foil and cook for a further 30 minutes. Discard the star anise.

▼ **VARIATION**

Dried prunes may be substituted for the figs.

Poached pears

Serves 6

Hands-on time: 10 minutes

Cooking time: 20–25 minutes

110 cals, trace fat (of which trace saturates), 27g carbohydrate per serving

300ml ($^1/_2$ pint) grape juice

50g (2oz) golden caster sugar

6 small firm pears

1 cinnamon stick

Zest of 1 organic orange

1 Put the grape juice and sugar into a pan and heat gently to dissolve the sugar. Add the pears, cinnamon stick and orange zest, cover, bring to the boil and simmer for 10–15 minutes until the pears are tender.

2 Transfer the pears to a bowl, discard the cinnamon stick and orange zest and bring the liquid to the boil. Simmer for 4–5 minutes until thick and syrupy. Serve the pears with the syrup poured over them.

Sweet toasted almonds

Scatter 200g (7oz) flaked almonds on a baking sheet and sprinkle 1 tbsp golden icing sugar over them. Put under a hot grill for 2–3 minutes until golden. Serve sprinkled over ice cream or baked fruit. Makes enough for six servings.

Roasted apples and oats with blueberries

Serves 4

Hands-on time: 15 minutes

Cooking time: 30–40 minutes

200 cals, 5g fat (of which 1g saturates), 39g carbohydrate per serving

4 Bramley apples

25g (1oz) pecan nuts

25g (1oz) organic oats

50g (2oz) blueberries

2 tbsp light muscovado sugar

4 tbsp orange juice

1 Preheat the oven to 200°C (180°C fan oven) mark 6. Core the apples, then use a sharp knife to score around the middle of each (this will stop the apple from collapsing). Put the apples in a roasting tin.

2 Chop the pecans and put in a bowl together with the oats, blueberries and sugar. Mix together, then spoon into the apples, pour the orange juice over them and cook in the oven for 30–40 minutes until the apples are soft.

Rhubarb and raspberry meringue

Serves 4

Hands-on time: 15 minutes

Cooking time: 10–15 minutes

90 cals, 3g fat (of which 0g fat saturates), 22g carbohydrate per serving

450g (1 lb) rhubarb

2.5cm (1in) piece stem ginger (optional)

Finely grated rind and juice of 1 organic orange

75g (3 oz) caster sugar

75g (3 oz) frozen raspberries

1 large egg white

1 Clean and cut the rhubarb into 2.5cm (1in) pieces. Finely chop the stem ginger, if using.

2 Place the rhubarb in a large saucepan with 25g (1oz) caster sugar, the chopped stem ginger, if using, and the orange rind. Cover and cook gently for 2–3 minutes, adding a little orange juice if necessary. Add the raspberries. Spoon the mixture into four 150ml (5fl oz) ramekins or ovenproof teacups.

3 Whisk the egg white and remaining sugar together until foamy. Place the bowl over a saucepan of simmering water and continue to whisk for 5 minutes or until stiff and shiny.

4 Place a spoonful of meringue mixture on top of each ramekin and bake at 180°C (160°C fan) mark 4 for 5-10 minutes or until lightly golden.

▼ COOK'S TIP

To prepare ahead complete the recipe to the end of step 2 up to 3 hours ahead of serving. Complete the recipe to use.

Apple and cranberry strudel

Serves 6

Hands-on time: 20 minutes

Cooking time: 40 minutes

140 cals, 3g fat (of which trace saturates), 29g carbohydrate per serving

700g (1$\frac{1}{2}$lb) red apples

1 tbsp lemon juice

2 tbsp golden caster sugar

100g (3$\frac{1}{2}$oz) dried cranberries

1 tbsp olive oil

6 sheets of filo pastry

1 Preheat the oven to 190ºC (170ºC fan oven) mark 5. Quarter, core and thickly slice the apples. Put in a bowl and mix with the lemon juice, 1 tbsp sugar and the cranberries.

2 Warm the oil in a pan. Lay 3 sheets of filo pastry side by side, overlapping the long edges. Brush with a little oil. Cover with 3 more sheets of filo and brush again. Tip the apple mixture on to the pastry and roll up from one longest edge. Put on a non-stick baking sheet, brush with the remaining oil and sprinkle with the remaining sugar.

3 Bake in the oven for 40 minutes or until the pastry is golden and the apples are soft.

Chocolate and prune pudding

Serves 6

Hands-on time: 10 minutes

Cooking time: 40 minutes

210 cals, 8g fat (of which 4g saturates), 26g carbohydrate per serving

600ml (1 pint) skimmed milk

2 large eggs

2 large egg yolks

40g (1½ oz) light brown sugar

½ tsp cornflour

2 tbsp cocoa powder, plus more for dusting

50g (2oz) plain chocolate, broken into tiny pieces

100g (3½ oz) ready-to-eat prunes, stoned

1 Preheat the oven to 170°C (150°C fan oven) mark 3. Heat the milk to simmering point. In a heatproof bowl, mix together the eggs, egg yolks, sugar, cornflour and cocoa. Add the broken chocolate, then slowly pour in the hot milk, stirring until it is combined and the chocolate has melted.

2 Put the prunes into the base of a serving dish or individual dishes, then strain in the milk mixture through a sieve. Put the dish in a roasting tin and fill the tin with boiling water so it comes halfway up the sides of the dish. Cook in the oven for about 30–40 minutes until just set.

3 Remove the dish from the tin and serve warm. Alternatively, leave to cool, then chill until ready to serve. Dust with cocoa before serving.

Almond macaroons

Makes 22

Hands-on time: 10 minutes

Cooking time: 12–15 minutes, plus cooling time

70 cals, 5g fat (of which trace saturates), 6g carbohydrate per macaroon

2 medium egg whites

125g (4oz) caster sugar

125g (4oz) ground almonds

$^{1}/_{4}$ tsp almond extract

22 blanched almonds

1 Preheat the oven to 180°C (fan oven 160°C) mark 4 and line several baking trays with baking parchment. Whisk the egg whites until stiff peaks form. Gradually whisk in the sugar, a little at a time, until thick and glossy. Gently stir in the ground almonds and almond extract.

2 Spoon teaspoonfuls of the mixture on to the prepared baking trays, spacing them slightly apart. Press an almond into the centre of each one and bake in the oven for 12–15 minutes until just golden and firm to the touch.

3 Leave on the baking sheets for 10 minutes, then transfer to wire racks to cool completely. Store in airtight containers or wrap in cellophane for a gift.

▼ **COOK'S TIP**

On cooling, these biscuits have a soft, chewy centre and harden up after a few days. Once made, eat within 1 week.

Mango and lime mousse

Serves 6

Hands-on time: 20 minutes, plus chilling time

Cooking time: none

230 cals, 12g fat (of which 6g saturates), 25g carbohydrate per serving

2 very ripe mangoes

100ml (3$\frac{1}{2}$fl oz) whipping cream

Finely grated zest and juice of 2 organic limes

10g ($\frac{1}{4}$oz) powdered gelatine

3 large eggs, plus 2 large yolks

50g (2oz) golden caster sugar

Finely pared organic lime zest, to decorate

1 Cut the mango flesh away from the stone and whiz in a blender or food processor to give 300ml ($\frac{1}{2}$ pint) purée. Lightly whip the cream in a bowl and set aside.

2 Put 3 tbsp lime juice in a small, heatproof bowl, then sprinkle with the powdered gelatine and leave to soak for 10 minutes.

3 In a large bowl, whisk together the eggs, egg yolks and sugar, using an electric beater, until thick and mousse-like; this will take about 4–5 minutes. Gently fold in the mango purée, cream and grated lime zest.

4 Set the bowl of softened gelatine over a pan of boiling water and leave until dissolved, then carefully fold into the mango mixture, making sure everything is evenly combined. Pour the mousse into glasses and chill for 2–3 hours until set. Decorate each mousse with shredded lime zest.

Banana and pecan muffins

Makes 12

Hands-on time: 15 minutes

Cooking time: 20 minutes, plus cooling time

220 cals, 12g fat (of which 4g saturates), 25g carbohydrate per muffin

100g (4oz) self-raising flour

100g (4oz) wholewheat self-raising flour

100g (4oz) buckwheat flour

75g (3oz) ground almonds

1 tsp baking powder

1 tsp bicarbonate of soda

3 large ripe bananas, about 450g (1lb),

   before peeling

125ml (4fl oz) apple juice

1 large egg, beaten

75g (3oz) butter, melted and cooled

50g (2oz) pecan nuts, toasted and roughly chopped

1 Preheat the oven to 180°C (160°C fan oven) mark 4 and line a muffin tin with 12 paper muffin cases. Sift the flours, baking powder and bicarbonate of soda together into a large mixing bowl and set aside.

2 Peel and mash the bananas in a bowl, using a fork. Add the beaten egg and melted butter and mix together until well combined. Add this to the flour mixture, together with the pecan nuts, and stir briefly; the mixture will be a lumpy paste.

3 Spoon the mixture into the muffin cases, then bake in the oven for 20 minutes or until they are golden and well risen.

4 Transfer to a wire rack to cool a little. Serve while still warm.

Ginger and fruit tea bread

Cuts into 12 slices

Hands-on time: 15 minutes, plus soaking time

Cooking time: 1 hour, plus cooling time

160 cals, 1g fat (of which trace saturates), 34g carbohydrate per serving

125g (4oz) each dried apricots, apples
  and stoned prunes, chopped

300ml ($^1/_2$ pint) strong fruit tea

A little butter for greasing

25g (1oz) stem ginger in syrup, chopped

225g (8oz) wholemeal flour

2 tsp baking powder

125g (4oz) dark muscovado sugar

1 egg

1 Put the dried fruit in a large bowl. Add the tea and leave to soak for 2 hours.

2 Preheat the oven to 180°C (160°C fan oven) mark 4. Grease and line the base of a 900g (2lb) loaf tin.

3 Add the remaining ingredients to the soaked fruit and mix thoroughly. Spoon into the prepared tin and brush with 2 tbsp cold water. Bake in the oven for 1 hour until cooked through.

4 Cool in the tin for 10–15 minutes, then turn out on to a wire rack to cool completely. Wrap in clingfilm and store in an airtight container. It will keep for up to three days.

Clafoutis

Serves 6

Hands-on time: 25 minutes

Cooking time: 1 hour

280 cals, 10g fat (of which 4g saturates), 39g carbohydrate per serving

350g (12oz) stoned cherries

3 tbsp kirsch

1 tbsp golden caster sugar

4 large eggs

100g (3$\frac{1}{2}$oz) caster sugar plus 1 tbsp.

25g (1oz) flour

150ml (5fl oz) milk

145ml (4$\frac{1}{2}$fl oz) single cream

1 tsp vanilla extract

1 Put the stoned cherries in a bowl with the kirsch and 1 tbsp golden caster sugar. Mix together, cover and set aside for 1 hour.

2 Meanwhile, whisk the eggs with the caster sugar and flour. Bring the milk and the cream to the boil and pour on to the egg mixture; whisk until combined. Add vanilla extract and strain into a bowl, cover and set aside for 30 minutes.

3 Lightly butter a 1.7-litre (3-pint) shallow ovenproof dish and dust with caster sugar. Spoon the cherries into the dish, whisk the batter and pour it over them. Bake at 180°C (160°C fan oven) mark 4 for 50–60 minutes or until golden and just set. Dust with icing sugar and serve warm with thick cream.

Contents

Useful contacts

Information about GI, and Low-GI diets in particular, can be found very easily by keying in 'information about Low-GI' on your web search engine. Supermarket web sites also contain good introductory information about GI diets and foods.

www.glycemicindex.com
Extremely informative and useful GI website, run by the University of Sydney's Glycemic Index Research Unit in Australia. Dr Jennie Brand-Miller, world authority on Low-GI eating and author of The New Glucose Revolution and the Low-GI Diet, is a member of the faculty.

Author acknowledgements

First and foremost, I should like to express my gratitude and profound thanks to my editor, Nicola Hodgson. No-one could have been gentler, more patient or more co-operative. I should also like to offer my very sincere thanks to Carly Madden for her support; and to Lorna Rhodes for sharing her knowledge on low-GI cooking so generously. On a personal level, for Joanna and Catey, for their unstinting support and affection, and for Stephanie, for her constant encouragement and good humour, my heartfelt thanks and love.

Photographer credits

Steve Baxter: 137

Linda Burgess: 6, 154

Will Heap:
31, 39, 47, 73, 93, 97, 105, 117, 125, 129, 141, 145, 153

Lucinda Symons: (Food Stylist: Sarah Tildesley) 2, 4, 8, 20, 23, 27, 35, 42, 51, 55, 59, 62, 65, 69, 75, 79, 85, 88, 112, 121, 132